SANTORINI

THIRASSIA

EDITIONS
TOUBI'S
ΕΚΔΟΣΕΙΣ

ATHENS 1998

© Copyright 1998   MICHAEL TOUBIS PUBLICATIONS S.A.
Nisiza Karela, Koropi, Attiki
Telephone: +30 210 6029974, Fax: +30 210 6646856
Web Site: http://www.toubis.gr

ISBN: 960-540-258-0

First page: coins of ancient Santorini, copperplate engraving by Gouffier.

Black ashes, carved rocks
stand, bolt upright, opposite
through erosion and time
and a dove, completely white,
pecks the hope

in your azure sky,
Thera, ship of primeval times
you sail, proud,
in the dark blue of the archipelago...

I. M. Chatziphotis

CONTENTS

CONTENTS

Santorini is not just an island; it has not developed as its island neighbours have. Its history, together with its people and their works, have been buried in the depths of the earth and born again –and not only once! It is for this reason that Santorini is unlike any other island. It is something exceptional; it is alone and lives in its own way. Even its people are different; they say of themselves, "we are not people, we are Santorinians". For this reason also, one cannot describe Santorini in the usual way. In order to describe it you have to look very hard and in doing so you will come to love and believe in the island. In order to convey the sense of uniqueness of the island, it is necessary to commune with the richness, history and geological sensitivity of the landscape.

Anyone who visits Santorini for the first time with some knowledge and experience of other Greek islands will certainly feel confused. Santorini is a very strange island, which has nothing in common with the rest of the Cyclades. They, taken as a whole, are like musical variations on the same theme. They give you a sense of harmony, calm and relaxation. All the lines, colours, sounds and styles are gentle. The other islands feel friendly, warm and tender as an embrace, whilst Santorini is neither calm nor gentle. On the contrary, it is wild and threatening; its shapes and colours are harsh. It thrusts up out of the sea like an immense chiaroscuro by Goya.

The whole island is one huge mound of volcanic lava. The ground is not part of the earth's crust, it was formed by the hardening of a viscous liquid which emerged, very hot, from the bowels of the earth –red, black and brown. The sea around it is 380 metres deep and is deepest darkest blue right to the water's edge. For a ship to drop anchor is impossible, the anchor would just hang loosely without finding land on which to grasp. A French traveller who, two centuries ago drew a map of the island, marked the sea with the nightmare word 'bottomless'.

The sea around Santorini conceals the abyss and in the middle of the sea floats the volcano –swarthy and lean like a crocodile's back.

An Island of Lava

A view of Santorini with the volcano. From 'The Illustrated London News', 31st March 1866, page 318.

Following Pages: Typical view of Thera. White and dark blue in an harmonic combination.

Once one has become aware of all of this, one is filled with awe, and it is this awe which is precisely the most valuable thing Santorini has to offer. In time, one recovers from the majesty, the picturesqueness, even the fear –but the awe remains, because you know that what is revealed before you are the bowels of the earth, the origin of us all. You know that here, with confidence and without shame, you can lay down all the myths you carry with you.

If we could choose two or three from among the many sights of Greece, we would undoubtedly choose Santorini among them. Such is the beauty of this island, with its wild beauty, eerie, burned by the forces of the volcano that lies in the middle of the bay of the island, like a black monster, sleeping half-submerged in the sea. Around it, like a crescent moon, the remains of the island which sank –a huge rock, multicoloured, black, red, grey, brownish. And on top of this rock, all around, the taming and appeasement of the wild and eerie landscape; the white crown with the houses, the arches, the terraces and the domed churches –Fira, Firostefani, Imerovigli and, further over, Oia. On the opposite side, on a little island, a remnant of the large island which was lost, is Thirassia. The presence of the people is intense; those who defied this wild monster and settled down up there bravely, provokingly. Was it ignorance of the danger that brought them to live on the edge of the cliff? Was it the wonder of the spectacular landscape, or the magnet of the breathtaking view which pulled them? The answer is difficult to know for certain.

Wild beauty and calmness in harmony with the eerie view that make up the landscape of the island.

Nature and Location

Together with Anafi, Santorini is the southernmost island of the Cyclades. It has an area of 96 square kilometres, a coastal length of 69 kilometres and its width varies from 2 to 6 kilometres. The ground of the island is volcanic and on the side of the volcano, the island is rocky and steep. Sheer, impressive cliffs and parallel layers of black and red rocks compose its western side.

In the southeast are the limestone masses of Mesa Vouno, with the highest summit being that of Prophitis Ilias (550 m). Gavrilos rises in the south, whilst in the north we find the peaks of Megalo Vouno and Mikros Prophitis Ilias.

The climate of the island is mild, Mediterranean. It is cool in the summer owing to the northeast winds (known as meltemia), and in the winter the weather is sweet and mild with an average temperature of 10°C. The rainfalls are frequent in winter but almost non-existent in summer.

The fertile earth of the island is good for the cultivation of vine as well as tomatoes which are very small but very delicious. Cucumbers and barley are also produced. Of the products from the island, the fava bean is well known. It is a pulse of exceptional quality but smaller than a dried pea. Also famous is the island's wine, especially the nychteri, or 'night wine' which is of an equally exceptional quality.

The island is almost waterless and has only a very few flowing springs. Consequently, the inhabitants often use rainwater for their everyday use. Today special water container trucks meet the water supply demands of the island.

The population of Santorini numbers some 11,400 people and the island is an administrative region of the prefecture of the Cyclades (the province of Thera). The people of Santorini are not only involved in farming but also in the exploitation of pumice. In recent years, of course, the development of tourism has meant that the people have turned to professions with a direct connection to the tourist industry.

Every year the island is visited by 500,000 people, tourists who remain astounded by its primeval beauty.

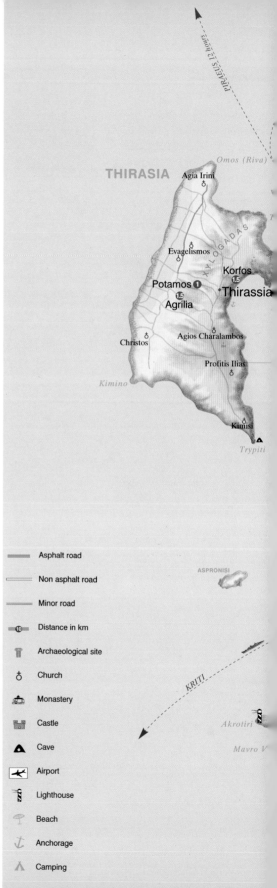

	Asphalt road
	Non asphalt road
	Minor road
⑩	Distance in km
	Archaeological site
⚲	Church
	Monastery
	Castle
▲	Cave
✈	Airport
	Lighthouse
	Beach
⚓	Anchorage
⋀	Camping

SANTORINI
(THIRA)

N

Mavropetra

Baxedes

BAXEDES

Kouloumbo

Agios Ioannis

Kyra Panagia

Tholos

APANO MERIA

Kouloumbos

Oia

Finikia

Perivolos

MAVRO VOUNO

Pori

Armeni

Mouzaki

Analipsi

Agios Artemios

BIRIKIA

Agia Irini

Theoskepasti

Imerovigli

Vourvoulos

Kanakari

ASPRA CHOMATA

Agios Nikolaos

Firostefani

Kontochori

Exo Gialos

Gialos

Karteradou

Tourlos

Firostefani

Mesa Katikies

MESIES

Fira (Thira)

TRYPES

Exo Katikies

MESA GIALOS

Karterados

Monolithos

NEA KAMENI

Monolithos

Agios Ioannis

THOLOS TILOS

Agia Paraskevi

Kamari

Alonaki

Agios Taxiarchis

Mesaria

Vothonas

Agia Paraskevi

Agios Nikolaos

KAMENI

Athinios

Exo Gonia

Mesa Gonia

Athinios

Pyrgos

Episkopi

Kamari

Megalochori

Panagia Gonias

PROFITIS ILIAS

CHROBILIA

Profitis Ilias
(Museum)

ARCHAEA
THIRA

Mesa
Vouno

Theoskepastá

Balos

MESA VOUNO

LOUMARADES

Akrotiri

Agios
Nikitas

Emporio

Agios Stavros
Zoodochos Pigi

Perissa

ADIA

AKROTIRI

Agia
Anna

DIAPLA

PERIVOLOS

Perissa

Agios
Nikolaos

Almyra

Akrotiri

Agios
Antonios

Ammos

Vlychada

GAVRILOS

Agios Georgios

Ai Giorgi

Vlychada

Exomitis

VLYCHADA

ELEFSINA

Exo Mytis

THE VOLCANO

The Volcano and its History

The geological history of Santorini begins many millions of years ago, at a time when Europe and Africa were still joined. At that time, what is today the Aegean Sea was a land mass known as Aegeis, which linked mainland Greece with Asia Minor and Crete.

After a long series of geological upheavals, Aegeis sank beneath the surface of the waves which rushed in to take its place. This must have happened about six million years ago. The mountain peaks of the old mainland remained protruding above the surface of the sea and are what, today, we call the islands the Aegean Sea. The position occupied today by Santorini had only two or three insignificant islets to show, which are still there today incorporated into the principal island. They are the mountain of Profitis Ilias, the rocks above the modern harbour at Athinios, and an isolated rock which stands proudly on the east coast of the island at Monolithos.

Even today it is not possible to know with absolute certainty and be absolutely sure about all the geological adventures Santorini has experienced. Many theories, hypotheses

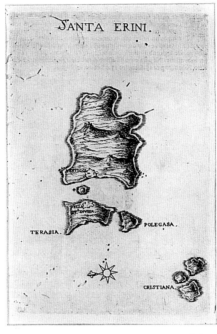

Map of Santorini by M. Boschini, Venice, 1654.

and interpretations exist which are all different but which agree in their significant points and thus help one to get a reasonably clear picture of the various phases of creation which helped to form 'the island of the devil'. The eruption of the volcano sent the greater part of Strongyle to the bottom of the sea and, at the same time, the whole area was drowned in myth! This myth travelled through time and took many names until its origins were lost. Other myths met with or came from it, such as, perhaps, the existence and sinking of Atlantis. Thus, today, nobody knows what to call these eighty four square kilometres of land disappeared to the bottom of the Aegean with a boom that could be heard to the ends of the earth.

The volcano first appeared around 80,000 years ago, the eruption was terrific. Ash found on the seabed and originating from this eruption covers an area stretching from Chios to Italy, and from North Africa almost as far as Cyprus. Of course, before it settled on the seabed, this ash must have darkened the skies over the area for a long time.

Apart from the ash, the crater expelled other, heavier substances which poured forth in liquid or semi-liquid form at great heat and formed a cone. This cone gradually grew, covering the surface of the sea, and joined with the islets already there to form an approximately circular island with a diameter of fourteen to fifteen kilometres.

It is not known how many centuries the island needed to assume its final form. What is known, however, is that around 2000 BC (the time when the Minoan civilization was reaching its peak on Crete), the island was inhabited by people who called it Strongyle (Round).

These people knew how to build two-storey houses, how to till the earth and produce olive oil and wheat. They had domesticated sheep and made cheese. They fished, wove and decorated their pottery, their houses and themselves. They were also very good with colours and were capable of producing wonderful paintings.

In order to get a clear picture of the life these people led, one must visit the archaeological dig at Akrotiri, where a complete town has been discovered under the ash.

The second catastrophic eruption happened relatively recently, around 1450 BC, and as a result all life on the island was obliterated. It appears that, directly beneath the centre of Strongyle, the flow of the lava created an enormous hollow dome which was eventually unable to support the weight of the island.

The roof of the dome collapsed and with it the greater part of Strongyle sank beneath the waves which rushed in to cover it. All that was left above the surface of the sea were parts of its perimeter, like open arms which enclosed a gigantic basin filled with the sea –the caldera. It is these arms which today are called Santorini, Thirassia and Aspronisi.

Eighty four square kilometres of ground collapsed and disappeared to the bottom of the sea, with a crash which must have been heard as far away as Norway. The Aegean was darkened by a vast black cloud of smoke and ash and an enormous tidal wave, 250 metres high, rose up and headed off at a speed of 350 kilometres an hour...

In less than half an hour it had reached Crete and, as many historians believe, drowned the entire Minoan civilization.

Map of the Mediterranean showing the extent of the eruption.

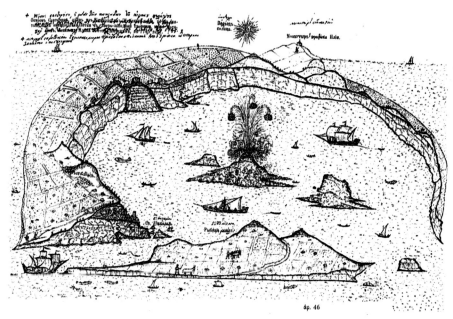

The island of Santorini with the active volcano, B. Barskij (IV, 152-3).

Olfert Dapper (1688).

The Volcano (198 BC - AD 1950)

Parallel with the people, the volcano continued its activity. From time to time, various craters erupted in the centre of the caldera which, although completely insignificant, nonetheless restarted the process of filling in the caldera. The lava formed cones around the crater, initially under the sea, which later projected above the surface and formed, in many successive phases, the two islands of **Palaia Kameni** and **Nea Kameni**, which are today simply called 'The Volcano'.

There were fourteen such eruptions between 198 BC and AD 1950. The eruption of 1650, which took place outside the caldera, six and a half kilometres from the northeast coast of Santorini at a place called Koloumbos, is described in the chronicle of the Jesuit Francois Richard. The cone which formed around this crater did not protrude above the surface of the sea and still exists today as a reef at a depth of 18.5 metres:

"On the night of the 27th of September, a new and more terrible earthquake made the houses reel hither and thither like babies' cradles and shook them like reeds in the wind. After this tremor, we saw, four miles to the east, between Andros and Santorini, flames wrapped in dense clouds leaping from the sea. A pall of smoke rose on high from the blazing abyss. Then the fiery clouds lowered upon us with a fearsome stench as if the flames were coming from Hell itself. Six days before, we had observed that the sea in that area was bright green in colour, a clear sign that the fire lurking in the depths was struggling to force open a cleft in the seabed and that sulphurous fumes were escaping into the water.

"In the two days which followed the flaring up of the flames, the ocean burned with an ever-increasing vigour, the earth tremors redoubled, the smoke grew ever thicker and the surface of the sea became covered with the pumice disgorged by the abyss.

"Notwithstanding this, our fear was nothing to what was to come on Sunday the 29th of September. This was the most terrible day of which history can speak. The sea growled menacingly, the earth quivered and the very air was afire. Thick sulphurous steam billowed out of the depths and rose on high as black clouds. Then suddenly the clouds caught fire, lightning rent the sky, thunder burst forth and strange forms moved before one's eyes: flying snakes, shining spears and lances and whirling blazing torches. All that day, the clouds hung low, the island shook and the wild elements met in such raging combat that their clamour could be heard a hundred leagues off. Ash fell as far away as Asia Minor. At Palatia, it covered the grapes on the unharvested vine. The ash was like white chalk or burned gypsum. The Turks said the islands were no more; fire from heaven had smitten them. It was observed by many that as the great peel of thunder rang out, the subterranean fire cast up into the heavens enormous rocks, which fell to earth again two leagues away. In a field we saw a boulder spewed from the bowels of the earth, of a size that forty men could not move it.

"Many of the islanders went stone blind for two or three days together. Their eyes gave them dire pain, they shrieked both day and night. Fifty souls and some thousand beasts were lost in this fell visitation, suffocated by the poisonous vapours. All the gold and silver objects enclosed within pouches or chests and all gilt and silvered things and embroideries turned black. The sacred vessels in the churches were altered in appearance, although they had been covered in their veils. Those icons which were unvarnished looked as if they had been completely obliterated, but the colours revived when washed with wine and vinegar. The silver objects too regained their lustre when burnished with oil and warm ash. Nine poor sailors, returning from Amorgos, their boats laden with wheat, came too close to the brim of the flaming chasm and were lost. Their charred bodies were found after three days and their boats drifted upon the sea with no hand at the tiller".

Fifty seven years later, in 1707, activity began in the centre of the caldera once more, being accompanied this time by the disturbing phenomenon of islands appearing where a short while before there had been only sea. These eruptions were described by Tarillon, another Jesuit, who happened to be in Santorini that year:

"...On the 18th of May, two minor earth tremors were experienced on the island. No one, however, paid any heed. It would appear that at that moment the islet began to rise up from the depths of the sea and to break through the surface of the waters. Whatever the truth of the matter may be, the sailors, seeing that morning the topmost points of the islet emerging, assumed that what they were seeing were the remains of a shipwreck that had taken place the previous night. They thus embarked in their boats and hastened to the spot to salvage what they might from the 'ship'. However, it was not a ship they encountered but rocks. The islanders in fear returned as fast as they might to port and told others of the strange sight they had seen".

Three days later, some of the bolder islanders approached the new islet in their boats and landed on it. But then...

"They suddenly felt the rocks begin to move and the ground upon which they were standing tremble. Dismayed, they abandoned the islet and made for their boats. This tremor was no more than a slight movement of the island as it grew. Within a few days it was twelve metres across and six metres high. Nonetheless, the island grew neither regularly nor in proportion. Many a time it would sink back at one point whilst swelling and spreading at another. One day, a huge rock emerged from the very middle of the reef and rose to a height of fifteen metres. I observed it carefully for four days. Suddenly it sank once more into the sea and was lost to view. There were rocks, too, which would sink for a few days, appearing and disappearing beneath the surface of the waters and in the end locked themselves into place. All these perturbations shook Mikri Kameni to its roots, and for the first time a deep crack appeared in its summit.

TABLE OF DATES OF ERUPTIONS

Number of eruption	Date	Interval between this and previous eruption	Changes in the form of the island
1	198-96 BC.		Palaia or Megali Kameni formed in successive phases (Mikri Kameni was formed in 1573).
2	19 AD.	215 years	
3	60	41 years	
4	726	666 years	
5	1457	731 years	
6	1508	51 years	
7	1573	65 years	Mikri Kameni, later to be incorporated into Nea Kameni, formed.
8	1650	77 years	Outside the caldera, in the sea to the NE of the island. No obvious change.
9	1707-12	57 years	The various fragments which gradually united to form the present-day Nea Kameni - the main bulk of the volcano - made successive apearances.
10	1866-70	154 years	
11	1925-26	55 years	
12	1928	2 years	
13	1940-41	12 years	
14	1950	9 years	Small successive eruptions.

"In the meantime the sea in the bay had been changing colour ceaselessly: from bright green to reddish and then to a light yellow. An oppressive odour rose from the depths of the water.

"Smoke was seen emerging from the new islet for the first time on the 16th of July. Not from that portion of it which was visible, however, but from a chain of black rocks which had emerged at a point where the sea until then had been bottomless. These rocks formed two separate islets, one of which was named **Aspronisi** (White Island) and the other **Mavronisi** (Black Island) owing to their colour. A little later, however, the two islets joined together, with the black rocks at their centre. Thick whitish smoke poured forth incessantly.

"On the night of the 19th to the 20th of July, flames were seen to spring from the midst of this smoke. The islanders of Skaros were seized with panic. Their houses stood but half a league away and the castle hung dizzily over cliffs which fell sheer into the sea. They expected that at any moment the fire, which must surely be creeping into the bowels of their own rock, would make an end of them. They decided to abandon the fortress and make with their belongings for another island of for another corner of Santorini. The Turks who chanced to be on the island to collect taxes were overcome with fear.

Beside themselves at the spectacle of the fire rising from the abyss, they exhorted the people to offer up prayers to God and urged the children to run out into the streets and cry "Lord have mercy on us", for, as they held, the innocent children, not yet having blasphemed against God as had their elders, retained their purity and might, by their prayers, appease the divine wrath.

"Nonetheless, the fire was not as yet worthy of mention, springing as it did from only one spot on Mavronisi and not being visible during the day.

Aspronisi seemed quiet: neither smoke nor fire. The other, however, grew constantly. Each day huge boulders could be seen coming to the surface: the island grew wider and narrower by turns and the boulders sometimes merged with the main island and sometimes drew away from it. Before a month was out there were four 'mavronisia' which then suddenly united to form one mass.

"The smoke grew thicker and thicker and, as the weather was windless, it rose so high that it could be seen from Crete, Naxos and other distant islands. There was a pillar of fire by night and on the sea floated a foam which was reddish in some places and yellowish in others. Then the clouds of smoke drifted so as to cover the whole of Santorini.

The islanders felt themselves suffocating and struggling for breath, and to keep down the fearful stench, they burned incense and lit fires in the streets. However, this lasted only two days. A strong sirocco sprang up and dispersed the smoke, which, however, in the meantime had passed over the vineyards and scorched the ripening grapes. Silver and copperware changed colour and tarnished. The people suffered from migraines and vomiting. The white island suddenly fell some three metres.

"On the 31st of July, the sea began to seethe at two circular spots, nine and eighteen metres from the black island. At these points the water burned like oil on a fire. The boiling lasted a month, and dead fish were washed up on the shore day and night.

"On the 1st of August, a deep reverberating booming was heard, as if cannons were being fired together far off. A little later, two flames sprang from the submarine furnace, soared high into the air and extinguished themselves.

"On the 17th of August, the islet began to spout jets of flame and the sea around it gave off smoke and boiled with foam. Fire poured from sixty or more orifices. The sea continued to be covered with that reddish foam which stank fearfully.

"Every night after the hollow roaring to which we had become accustomed, lambent tongues of fire could be seen springing from the sea's depths, with millions of lights which shot up into the heavens and then fell back like a rain of stars upon the island, itself all aglow.

"As the fire disported itself, another strange

Thick smoke rising from the crater of Nea Kameni during the eruption of 1926.

phenomenon took its turn to strike awe into the islanders. Amidst the flames winging through the air, one tongue of fire detached itself and hung high and attenuated for some time over the fortress of Skaros. As the hearts of the islanders rose into their mouths at this evil omen, the tongue of fire sprang still higher and was lost among the clouds.

"On the 9th of September, the two islands joined to become one solid mass. Only four of their 60 craters continued to vomit fire. Smoke and flames were belched forth from these openings, sometimes with thunderous noises and sometimes with wild whistling sounds, reminiscent of the howling of beasts.

"The submarine rumblings died down somewhat after the 12th of September. All that was heard from time to time was thunder like massed artillery fire. Now and then huge incandescent stones were thrown up out of each crater. The clouds of smoke became whirlwinds and an endless rain of ash fell upon the island. The eruptions gained force once more after the 18th of September. The boulders emitted from the craters collided with each other in the air with fearful crashes. Then they would fall back on Santorini or splash into the sea. Mikri Kameni often seemed completely covered by these incandescent boulders and glowed at night.

"On the 21st of September, Mikri Kameni was all alight. Suddenly three thunderbolts lit up the horizon from end to end. The new island was shaken to the depths; it quaked and shuddered from side to side. One of the craters sank and vast boulders were hurled to a distance of three miles. Four days of calm followed before the pandemonium broke loose once more. The explosions were continuous and so loud that two persons shouting to each other face to face were unable to hear what the other said. People hastened in panic to the churches. The Skaros rock could be seen to undulate and the doors of the houses banged open of their own accord. The eruptions did not stop at all until February 1708. On the 10th of February, the volcano let loose again. Mountainous rocks were spewed forth from the crater, the island shook, subterranean rumbling filled the heart with fear and the sea boiled. There was an explosion every two minutes. The flames could now be seen by day for the first time. This inferno continued until the 23rd of May. The new island spread and gained height ceaselessly. Lava extended the great crater. Then, at last, all was calm".

What happened in 1956 was not an eruption but an earthquake which destroyed everything on the island.

MYTHS & HISTORY

Mythology - Ancient Times - Byzantine Period - Frankish Occupation

Reliefs and wall paintings, elements which form the myth and history of the island.

The history of Santorini is not just the history of people. It is the history of a place which has the unrealistic distinction of constantly evolving and taking shape by itself. In order to understand this, try thinking back an Aegean with the Cyclades but without Santorini. Then imagine the island one day emerging from the seabed, rising, drying out and gradually being inhabited to become the home of a major culture. Next, picture another day on which half the island founders, taking its people and their achievements with it under the ashes and the waves. When the turmoil dies down, new inhabitants come to the island, give it a name of their own and start again from the beginning. Now imagine another island rising from the sea, little by little, and taking the place of that which sank...

The history of Santorini is the history of a place which is not to be taken for granted and whose map must, from time to time, be scrapped and redrawn from the start.

The first inhabitants of Santorini were pre-Hellenes who arrived around 3000 BC. The influence from Minoan Crete became clear when the excavations at Akrotiri began and an entire settlement with two-storey houses containing wall paintings similar to those of the Minoan palaces, was revealed beneath a thick layer of volcanic ash. When this settlement was built, the island was called Calliste (Most Charming) or Strongyle (Round) because of its shape –the volcano had not yet begun its catastrophic upheavals.

Mythology

The facts pertaining to the events leading up to the second eruption of the volcano, though absolutely proved today, are not mentioned, even as a memory, in any of the ancient texts. It is only in the ancient Greek myths and in the symbolism of the Old Testament that one encounters the echo of terrible disturbances of nature in the Mediterranean about fourteen of fifteen centuries before the birth of Christ; disturbances which must, at least as hypotheses, be related to the eruption of Santorini around 1450 BC. Thus, it is not impossible that the myth of Deucalion and Pyrrha, the sole survivors of the flood sent by Zeus to punish mankind, may well be directly connected to the eruption of Santorini. This flood can be placed chronologically between 1530 and 1400 BC.

Another relevant flood myth is that concerning Poseidon, who in anger swamped Attica when he lost the contest with Athena over which of them was to be sovereign in Athens. The death of Hippolytus was also the result of a giant wave raised by Poseidon near Troezen. Finally, ten or fifteen years at most before the death of Hippolytus, Theseus had relieved the Athenians of their tribute to Crete. Could the truth of the matter be that the state of Minos no longer existed?

In the Old Testament, it is not an unfeasible hypothesis that the plagues of Egypt were a result of the eruption which reached the land of the Pharaohs. Huge amounts of iron oxides must have turned the waters of the land red, whilst sulphur compounds must have poisoned all life and the flaming volcanic ash burned the vegetation.

Ancient Times

After the total destruction, calm came once more. Hesitantly at first, the people and then the volcano began to resume their normal routine. Of the first settlers who dared to land on the island, all we know is what can be concluded from the myths. It seems that the Phoenicians were first drawn here by the beauty of the landscape around 1300 BC. They colonized the island and gave it the name Calliste. Towards the end of the 12th century BC, possibly in 1115, more colonists arrived. These were Dorians from Lacedaemonia and were accompanied by their king, Theras, son of Autesion and great-great-great-grandson of Oedipus. The name of the island changed again, to become Thera, and harbours, towns and sanctuaries were built. In 825 BC, the Phoenician alphabet was introduced to Thera. In 630 BC, Theran colonists abandoned the island in despair after a long period of drought and founded Cyrene on the north coast of Africa. Some time later, we find Thera as an ally of the Lacedaemonians and still later as a tax-paying subject of Athens. In the Hellenistic period, it was a naval base for the Ptolemies and from this period there survives a complete town, Ancient Thera at Mesa Vouno (see Archaeological Sites). Both the sovereignty of the Ptolemies and the role of Santorini as a base ended with the Roman conquest.

View of ancient Thera.

Byzantine Period

Santorini was converted to Christianity in the 3rd century AD and became the see of a bishop, the first being Dioscorus (347 - 344). From the time of Justinian, the bishopric of Thera, along with eleven others, was placed under the administration of Rhodes. The most significant Byzantine monument is the elegant little church of Panagia Episkopi Gonia built by the Emperor Alexius I Comnenus (1081 - 1118) on early Christian ruins. A Byzantine museum has recently opened in Pyrgos, which hosts icons and other relics of Byzantine art from the churches of the town. The museum was organized by, and functions under the care of, the Second Trusteeship of Byzantine Antiquities.

1. The Byzantine icon from the church of Episkopi Gonia.
2. The church of Episkopi Gonia.

A view of Oia. Engraving on copper (drawing J. B. Hilaire).

The Frankish Occupation and Subsequent Years

The Franks came to Thera in 1204. They named the island Santorini and made the fortress of Skaros their capital. From this time, a period of misadventures began for the inhabitants of the island. There were disputes between the dukes of Naxos and the dukes of Santorini, attempts on the part of the Byzantine Empire to liberate the island, Turkish raids, outbursts of murderous jealousy between Genoa and the Serene Republic of Venice, but it was the islanders who paid for everything. Only on one occasion did the island change hands peaceably when, in 1480, the duke of Naxos gave it as dowry to his daughter who was marrying the duke of Crete. However, even that did not last long, for the bride's uncle disagreed and when he came to power he took the island back. Things calmed down noticeably when Santorini became part of the Ottoman Empire in 1579. However, so many centuries of internal turmoil, along with the damage inflicted by the corsair raids, had decimated the population –it is unlikely that there were more than five hundred inhabitants at this time. The Turks did not colonize the island, it seems only that they were impressed by the windmills they found there and consequently called Santorini, Deyrmetcik *(Little Mill)*. In all other respects, the island lived with relative autonomy and the inhabitants themselves elected their headmen who represented them before the Ottoman authorities. The Catholics lived on Skaros around their bishop, whilst the Orthodox lived with their bishop in the other fortresses and villages of the island. As piracy gradually died out, the island began to recover, to engage in trade and to acquire its own fleet. In 1821, the fleet of Santorini was the third largest in Greece, after those of Hydra and Spetses, with 5,000 tons. By 1852, Santorini had fallen back to fifth place, although its fleet had doubled in size. At this time, Syros, Spetses, Galaxidi and Hydra had larger fleets. After Santorini came Piraeus in sixth place. A rich source of information on the period of the Turkish occupation can be found in the chronicles of foreign travellers. In a chronicle he published in Paris in 1657, the French Jesuit, Francois Richard, gives a clear picture of the inhabited regions of the island in the mid 17th century:

"*In Santorini there are five towns or pyrgi [fortified places]. The first is called Kastro and enjoys the respect of all [he means Skaros]. It was there that the dukes and governors of the island lived before it became subject to the Turks. It was also the site of the ducal palace. Today, Kastro is the seat of the Latin bishop.*

"*Kastro stands at a great height and it takes half an hour to reach its walls. Its gates used to be closed when enemy attack was feared. There used to be two hundred houses on the cliff which rises in its very centre. These have now been abandoned and little by little are being pulled down. No one now has any wish to live at such a height. It was with the stones of the ruined houses that they built their church. It is said that at the top of the cliff there used to be a great bell to warn the people whenever a corsair ship appeared in the sea. At the present time, when danger threatens they light beacon fires as they do on other islands.*

"*The name of the second fortress is Pyrgos. It stood in the middle of its little town and was used by the inhabitants as a place of refuge in wartime. This is where the cadi who came to the island every two years to administer justice used to stay. But since the outbreak of the Ottoman-Venetian War, the Venetians had control of the sea and held hostage all the Turks of the Aegean islands and permit no new Ottoman settlements. Nowadays (18th century) the island is governed by the headmen who must pay tax both to the Sultan and to the Serene Republic of Venice. The third fortified place is called Emboreio, that is to say Market. This is where the sale of all merchandise takes place. The other two fortresses are situated at the two extremes of the islands: one at Apano Meria and the other at Akrotiri. There are also many villages: Karterados, Messaria, Megalo Chorio and others. Karterados, apart from the Greeks, has two hundred Catholics*".

1. Engraving of Skaros, by Thomas Hope (1769-1831).
2, 3. The castle of Oia.
4. The castle of Emboreio.

CULTURE & TRADITION

Manners & Customs - People & Occupations - Architecture

The earthquake did not damage only the buildings. It demolished a whole epoch and buried it for ever. This out-of-the-way, half-forgotten island, southernmost of the Cyclades, was suddenly a name on everyone's lips, front page news, first item on the agenda, the apple of the state's eye, bustling with people and activity: social security agencies, stretcher bearers, civil servants, workmen, engineers, architects, buildings sites, compensation, grants and speculation. At the same time though, - and this is not the first peculiar thing about Santorini- the earthquake was

Tradition and evolution. A new era begins on the island, connected to the roots of the past.

responsible for unearthing a considerable proportion of the island's population. At least half the islanders must, up to that time, have been living out of sight in the houses known today as skafta and shown off as traditional forms of housing. All these people came out on to the surface for once, got a taste of the sunshine and new houses which were built on top of the ground as opposed to being dug out of it, and gradually came to realise that they were now the owners of ruins that were beginning to acquire considerable value. All in all, what happened was that immediately after the earthquake, the locals and the imported talent set

about putting the island back on its feet. The first thing needed of course was some kind of rudimentary infrastructure. Among the first measures to be implemented were electrification, the extension of the island's primitive road network and the construction of a new harbour which would be accessible not only to ships but also to wheeled transport on the island. There followed the telephone, an airport and finally the cable-car. All these improvements brought about earth-shattering changes on the island, but the islanders, accustomed to literally earth-shattering upheavals, reacted with utter calm and a good deal of philosophy: "Earthquake? So what?". This in turn means that when they started laying the foundations over the ruins of their island, they knew somewhere in the depths of their souls, that they would be building a new era. It was tourism which gave this new era its character. In the beginning there were some far-sighted foreigners who started buying up ruins, re-building them –with every respect for the local style of architecture– and using them for their own purposes or as rented properties. These first pioneers were followed by more far-sighted foreigners and they by yet more.

In the end, of course, the Greeks also woke up, realized that there was money to be made in this business and rolled up their sleeves. In their turn, they began to buy up ruins and rebuild them.

White specks began to appear here and there against the grey background of the ruins. In the end, the whole place became white again, with only the occasional grey speck to bear witness to the catastrophe.

In the meantime, travel to and from the island had become easier, supply difficulties were overcome and the tourists started to arrive.

The islanders were initiated into the science of the rented room. After all, a place with so many natural attractions needs very little to turn itself into a magnet for tourists.

Thus, the question of what the islanders of Santorini do about work today has a self-evident answer: tourism is the main occupation. In the summer, the island is swamped by visitors, life takes place in the open air and the locals work flat out. When winter comes, everything goes dead, the people shut themselves up in their houses and catch up on lost sleep. In the spring, before the tourists start to arrive, the island is a hive of activity as preparations are made and everything is repainted and freshened up.

None of this, however, is of particular interest to us; there is nothing new or extraordinary about it and, more importantly, it does not reflect the real face of the island. Perhaps if we are to find that, we will have to go back into the recent past, about forty years back.

There are many reasons why this restrospective is a good idea: First of all, the people who lived in the years before the earthquake are the Santorinians we meet when we visit the island. They are the ones whom we will want to get to know and understand. No matter how large the changes in their lives over the last thirty years have been, no matter how different their daily round may be today, there must surely be something left of the individuality of a race who once boasted, "we are not people, we are Santorinians".

Another reason is to try to understand why the Santorinians occupied themselves so much

It is the old who pass the traditions to the new generation.

with tourism. According to the prevailing perception, tourism provides direct financial benefits –and considerable ones at that– but is also disastrous from a cultural point of view. At least tourism as we know it in Greece. Here we shall not examine if this perception is valid or not.

What is of interest to us is that one result of this concept is the constant expression of pious wishes that cultural identity can be maintained, that something will survive. These wishes are accompanied by nostalgia, disillusion, pessimism, anger and –much more rarely– by activities aimed at getting something done. Let us stop for a moment at the anger and censure those islanders who found themselves a source of easy profit and turned their backs on everything else. None of them can know what poverty means. Poverty means having nothing, absolutely nothing, no salary, no income, not a day's work nor any hope; things we associate today with other centuries, or other continents.

The Santorinians had a word for it: dystychame, expressive not only of misery itself but also of its permanence and limitlessness. The word was indicative of a different order of people, people who had families of twelve, sixteen or eighteen children, and who counted themselves fortunate when war came along and carried off half the children allowing the others to live, brutal times. The land of course is fertile and its produce is top quality, although there is some lack of variety. Some of the staples –flour, potatoes, olive oil and meat– are imported and have to be paid for. And then who owned the fields anyway? How many more hands would be needed to till them? The father, a boatman, had work once a week and the boat wasn't his. The mother, a cleaner, waited for the summer for a local living in Athens to come to the island for a couple of months' holiday so she could earn a wage or two. There were eight children in the house until the oldest girl grew up –that is reached the age of twelve– and could be sent off to Athens to go into service.

The servant girl in her turn would spend all winter saving her wage so as to be able, before 'going down' for the summer, to buy shoes for her brothers and sisters –all very reminiscent of a nineteenth century novel. What this does not mean, however, is that the sudden passage from wretchedness to comfort has not been without its price. The nostalgia we were talking about above is not simply a matter of sentiment.

It conceals awareness of a very specific danger: that everything will be lost, everything will be forgotten, we shall be left rootless. What is in question is not progress, evolution and change, that would be ludicrous, for the world has never ceased to evolve. What is in question, however, is memory –the thoughtless destruction of memory. For memory is culture. Why on earth should evolution be cognate with destruction? Why on earth should we abuse memory? A smooth road must exist...maybe one day the Greeks will find a right way to cherish memory.

Manners and Customs

Influence from western elements had, and has, various cultural effects on the island which are to be encountered where one least expects them. Who would have imagined that the islanders of Santorini would make Christmas pudding just like the English? The name has been corrupted of course, to the French-sounding bouden, but the recipe and taste are the same. They also make nioki, which is Italian. Then there are the names of the people: Sarlos, Virzini, Flora, Guillaime or the more Greek, Gulielmos, Klotidi (or Klotinda in dialect). There were even French nicknames: there was the boatman known, perhaps maliciously, as Loudeme, from loup de mer, or sea wolf. Besides these western names, it is not impossible for one to find Russian ones among them: Annushka, Kolias... which presumably arrived along with the samovars. Of course there were also the local names, that is to say the Greek names for which the locals had a preference: Minas and Markos for the men, Maroulidi or Maroulio for the women. The language of Santorini, however, even if influenced by western elements, has kept its identity.

Also, throughout the year many feasts and festivals are organized, mainly of religious character, which show the vivid religiousness of the people of Santorini. Characteristic is the celebration of the Panagia, on the 15th of August, at Akrotiri, Kamari and Megalochori, with music and dancing which present the real picture of the island and its inhabitants. The songs of the Santorinians which are sung at feasts and celebrations, are another element of the identity of the island. The celebrations are usually held in the morning and include food and, more rarely, dancing and singing. At the celebration connected with them, each saint has a dish of their own from which they take their name. Agios Georgis Sfoungatas, for instance, is celebrated by the making of a sfoungato (omelette). As throughout the Cyclades, the Santorini dance is that known as the ballos and, of course, the islanders play instruments –the lute and violins which they call paichnidia (toys).

Male and female costumes of Santorini. Drawing by Y. Crasset, Paris 1806. From the collection of Em. Lignou.

What is unique among the Santorinians however, is the island song, a couplet set to a local melody and full of the ancient and unrequited passion for love and wealth.

Lastly, there are those couplets which the islanders sing at every moment of their lives, whether they be muleteers walking up from Gialos in the blazing heat, or revellers returning home at night, and which are heard despite the pangs of hunger or the threat of earthquakes. There is one couplet which all the Greeks since the time of the Persian Wars and perhaps earlier must have sung:

Patience, patience, wait around,
This difficult climb will one day go down.

Only belief of this kind can explain why this place is still on its feet.

The religious festivals in honour of a saint show the deep religiousness of the people of Santorini but also their cheerful spirit because they are accompanied by dances and singing.

People and Occupations

In order to fully understand the occupations of the inhabitants, it must be understood that the villages are a long way from the sea. Fira, the main town, is half an hour from the nearest beach. Until a few years ago there was not one coastal village on the entire island –just a couple of houses at Kamari and perhaps the same number again at Perissa. The villages which stand at Kamari and Perissa today were basically built by the tourists. Very few of the islanders were fishermen and most of them were unable to swim. As for those who, in former days came as holiday-makers to Santorini, they only swam a few times the whole summer. It is not difficult therefore, to understand the situation. Simply take away the cars from Santorini as it is today and imagine most of the people living in Fira, Imerovigli, A-pano Meria and Pyrgos. The sea was inaccessible and foresight, organization and planning were needed to go swimming at Kamari. The party would have to be made to agree on a date, the wind would have to be not too strong and the muleteers would have to be notified to bring the right number of mules. Then the whole caravan would set off –around two hours to get there and the same amount to get back. Of course, at Kamari, it was deserted.

Thus, the Santorinians lived on the top of their island and most of them were farmers, using their donkeys and mules for work and as a means of transport. There were very few horses which have lost their once predominant role as beasts of burden and the muleteers –second most important profession on the island– would certainly have taken up other similar professions if these same animals did not take part in the festivals. When the cruise ships land, the passengers disembark at the old harbour, at Mesa Gialos, and the visitor uses the traditional means of transport to get themselves up to Fira –cable-car or no cable-car.

Pictures of a traditional way of life that is disappearing.

These animals are, one might think, the only ones on the island. The others, what we might call the 'stock-breeding' animals, are nowhere to be seen. Indeed one could claim that they did not exist at all if it were not for the small amounts of goat's-milk cheese (known as chloro, fresh), made at Pyrgos and Gonia and the sausages produced in the same villages. Both cheese and sausages are very hard to find but worth spending the time to look.

The land is fertile. This earth which, when it is windy is blown up in a dust as thin as pepper and blinds you, appears to work miracles. There can be no other explanation for the quality of its produce, especially as on this barren island, watering is not possible. The most important crop is the **grape**. It is said that it is the same variety which was once cultivated at Monemvassia and from which the legendary Malmsey wine was made, cuttings of which were taken and planted on Cyprus and Santorini when the vineyards there were abandoned. The truth of the matter is that here you will find many varieties of grapes: Assyrtico, Aedapi, Athiri, Mandylaria, Vaftra and Eftakilo, all of the finest quality –as is the wine made from them which today you buy bottled under various different names. In the past, the only types of wine known were the brusco, Bordeaux, the nychteri (or 'night wine') and the sweet red wine from the sundried grapes called visanto –from vino sancto, or Communion wine. All the wine was home produced. You went with your demijohn to Evangelou's cellar or to the Dominicans –huge vaulted cellars beneath the largest mansions, like underground railway stations. To the right and left would be the barrels, the casks and at the far end the wine press. In front of this would stand the two tanks in which the must was gathered. The cellars really came to life just after the feast of Panagia, on the 15th of August. This was when the grape harvest began, the ventema, and during which the island was a hive of activity. The animals went back and forth all day from the vineyard to the cellars, each carrying two large baskets full of grapes.

The volcanic soil of the island is fertile.
The island's inhabitants are hardworking and friendly
so don't be surprised if somebody offers you a glass of wine
from his new production.

The vineyards were harvested all day by both men and women whilst, at the same time in the cellars there were usually only men with their trouser legs rolled up a little higher than normal, their hands clasped behind their backs and their bodies leaning forwards a little as they rhythmically trampled the grapes. One can imagine what fun the trampling of the grapes was for the children –there was nothing to compare with the ticklish feeling on the soles of the feet as one trod, not to mention the literally intoxicating atmosphere produced by the fumes. The only slightly unpleasant sensation was to stand in the footprint just made by someone else and which was still warm. One of the Santorini wines was made from untrodden grapes: the last loads brought each evening by the muleteers and which would be trampled next morning, lay all night heaped in the press, which caused the grapes to burst from their own weight. The juice was collected in a special container and from it the nychteri was made. Most of the cellars survived the earthquake and are easy to visit as they have been made into restaurants and bars, and there are still some people who cultivate the vine. Perhaps someone will have the idea of taking a few cuttings and planting them somewhere else, as happened with the Malmsey vineyards all those centuries ago. If one excepts the grape, and the barley which is grown as animal food, there is something strange about all the other agricultural products of Santorini. Take the tomatoes for instance, the second most important crop on the island. The size of marbles we played with as children, their skin is tough and their taste unbelievable. You would think that someone had managed to condense into this tiny mass, all the taste of a large tomato. The purée, of course, which was made from these tomatoes, is of the same quality and is called berdes by the locals. Before the earthquakes, there were nine factories on the island making berdes and canning it. Now they are abandoned –the earthquake, one might think. However, the chimneys are still standing. How to explain it then? The blame falls on the fact that there are no more tomatoes.

The tomatoes are so small as to be difficult to pick, but it's worth the effort.

There is only one factory left, belonging to the Co-operative, and during the harvest season it works only one day in three. To put it another way, tomato production today has fallen by a factor of 27, or by 96%. Santorini is famous for its **fava** which, however, lately belongs to its rare products. It is a pulse, smaller than a dried pea, like a large grain of sand. Though very few, the island also produces vegetables such as cucumbers –known as katsounia– which are short, thick, stripey and have a fuzz. The aubergines are white and there are also white water melons (the flesh, not its skin) with jet-black pips. From what we have seen so far, it is clear how difficult it is for one to find on Santorini the things which are normally considered traditional –wood carvings, cloth, pottery or iron work. The reason, of course, is that these are always used for the local things. There is a little basket-weaving with wicker, the baskets that the animals carry and those things like muzzles that they put over the snouts of the mules. One may come across the odd hand grinder for the fava or wooden utensils which they use in the wine cellar, or perhaps a stone pestle and mortar. That is all.

*Two different roles: the wife at home
and her husband in trade.*

Architecture

Most of the islanders used to live in houses dug into the earth. This way around the housing problem was a consequence of the morphology of the ground, its composition, the lack of building materials and the very serious problem of transporting them.

If one looks at Santorini from a distance, it will be seen that the island seems to consist of masses of land rising more or less vertically out of the sea. There are no slopes, only cliffs. The land masses are arranged vertically above, and a little behind, one another. The overall appearance is that of land rising in gigantic terraces which are higher then they are deep. Even the back side of the island, which descends more gently towards the sea, descends in terraces.

On the other hand, the ground or at least the topsoil, consists of a kind of firm whitish sand. The mixture is made up of volcanic dust, earth and ash and has the advantage of being easy to dig whilst being solid enough not to collapse (most of the houses which survived the earthquake were skafta). These two factors combined to provide the islanders with the simplest of solutions: they dug a horizontal tunnel in the ground, built a wall across the mouth, and moved in. This solution had not only the beauty of simplicity but also the force of necessity, for the island has none of the usual building materials: there is no clay for bricks, there are no trees for timber and, most important of all, there is no water. All there are, are stones of a type impossible to work and there is no trace of the schist rock formations which would allow traditional dry-stone techniques to be employed. Thus the skafta came into being: long narrow passages with vaulted ceilings. The entrance was the only point of access for fresh air and light and because of this, there were a number of openings in the wall across it: the door, with a large light directly above and windows to the right and left.

How did the builders, without specialist knowledge or suitable materials, manage to create practical houses of high aesthetic appeal?

The house was divided into two communicating rooms by a wall parallel to that across the entrance, of which, in fact, it was an exact copy. In this way, the inner room, the bedroom, also received light. Sometimes there was a third room, which was used as a storeroom and was called the skoteino (dark room). The front room was the parlour.

In truth, the above description is somewhat schematic. The rock face was never exactly vertical and a part of the house usually protruded for a short distance beyond the mouth, but rarely far enough to allow windows to be incorporated into the sides of this extension. In front of each house was always a courtyard. This was absolutely essential. Around it stood the tiny kitchen, the privy and perhaps a henhouse. The water cistern, which was dug into the yard, served to collect the water channelled to it from the yard which collected the rainwater either directly or via the roof. The outsides of the houses were not usually whitewashed, except for the roofs which were in order to keep the rainwater clean. The fronts of the houses were the colour of their plaster –a very light whitish ash colour– whilst the plaster in its turn was decorated with reddish or greyish black pebbles pressed into it at random intervals. This method of decoration is still used today when houses are being restored, although it is all to obvious that it is copied. Perhaps what is to blame is the fact that they add large amounts of cement to the plaster mix. Or maybe a certain degree of symmetry in the placing of pebbles is the problem. Whatever it may be, something tells you that what you are seeing is not authentic. The houses themselves were not as nightmarish as one might expect, bearing in mind the idea of a skafta, which be seen by the fact that today they fetch high prices, are put back in order and people live in them comfortably.

Apart from the skafta there were also the houses of the rich which were built on the flat open ground at the summits. They were large, stone built and plastered, and were sometimes even painted outside with a faint ochre. Their doors and windows were flanked by carved limestone or marble. Above the main entrance of the courtyard there was always a pediment, also of marble, bearing the owner's initials and the date the house was constructed. These were not simply houses, but mansions, with as many rooms for the rich as the poor had children; eighteen, twenty, twenty two,... and with yards all around, cellars underneath for the wine, stables and byres for the animals, the orchards further back and the fields behind them stretching as far as Exo Gialos and the sea. In one of these houses, the gardener's hut still survives in a deserted corner of the old garden, as do the painted decorations which adorned the ceiling. Most of these mansions, however, have collapsed or were abandoned after the earthquakes as being unsafe and have gone to ruin. In Oia, one can see ruins of the houses of the old ship-owners, whilst two mansions still stand in Messaria and at Fira there is one which has been repaired and is still lived in –across from the museum. How did the Santorinians once get rich? through shipping, naturally, and through trade. The men travelled to the four corners of the earth and this can be seen if one goes inside any of the old mansions: Viennese furniture, Venetian mirrors, English china and even samovars. Another element of tradition is the way in which the Santorinians build their houses. What is characteristic of the villages as a whole is that there are no signs of straight lines or symmetry. Not even the vaults are symmetrical. It is enough for one to glance at the walls on the cliff side of the roads and you will see that, unless they have been built recently with concrete blocks and cement, none of the walls are the same thickness along their length. This plethora of asymmetrical, wiggly lines, meeting to form the most unlikely shapes, is what gives to the masses of the buildings, a sweetness and gentleness that are surprising on such an island. It would seem that, without really intending to, the islanders have given their home precisely what nature had deprived it of –tenderness.

Besides the skafta houses there were also mansions which stood out for their richness, but unfortunately most of them are ruins.

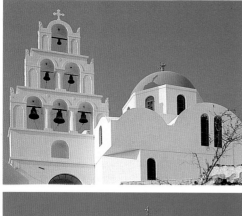

Ecclesiastical Architecture

The churches are out of all proportion to the humble masses which form the villages. They occupy a great deal of space, are imposing and, irrespective of whether they are Orthodox or Catholic, combine both local and western architectural elements. Some are completely white, others painted ochre. Some are basilicas, others in the form of a Byzantine cross. They very often have domes and two bell-towers in the façade like old-style cathedrals. The domes are dazzling white or light blue emulsion or even a light azure. Finally, the architecture of the Catholic monasteries is very special. Really fortresses, they are massive, strongly built with internal yards and arches and are always painted ochre.

Domes and bell-towers. Examples of a great architecture but also of deep devotion.

FIRA

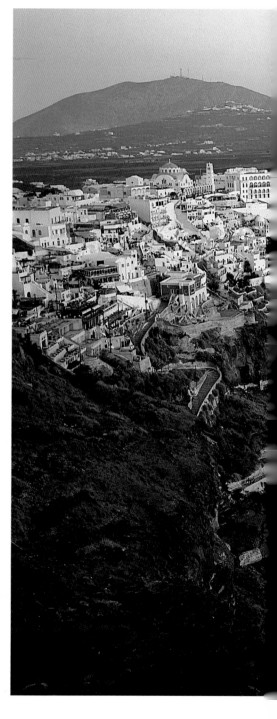

Fira is built on the edge of the vertical cliff, 260 metres above the sea. The combination of the wonderful landscape with the volcano and the famous Cycladic architecture makes Fira one of the most wonderful places on earth. The town is reached by car after ten kilometres from Athinios, the port where the ferries dock or from the little bay of Fira on foot or by donkey, using the picturesque cobbled street which ascends drawing a white zig-zag line on the rock. However, if you prefer it more comfortable and modern, then you can use the cable-car to get up. It is true that the development, the crowds of people and the noise have changed the local colour quite a lot, but the walk through the narrow alleyways of Fira will be a unique experience. The white houses with their arches, the terraces and the balconies with the wonderful view, the domed churches, the tavernas, the bars and the shops all crowded with people will charm you. You can visit the archaeological museum which hosts important finds from Akrotiri and Ancient Thera. You can also visit the old Catholic convent of the Dominican Nuns, and the Orthodox and Catholic Cathedrals. Fira is the capital of Santorini with a cathedral, a high school, banks, hotels, a medical centre and art galleries. The capital is among Santorini's relatively new settlements, with barely two centuries of life behind it. It was created in the late 18th century when circumstances no longer obliged the islanders to live high up on the inaccessible parts of the islands. At that time Skaros was still the most important fortified place. However, its inhabitants began to look around for somewhere else to live, in a flatter spot with some sort of access to the sea. Skaros was gradually abandoned and the new capital created.

There has been much controversy over the origin of the name 'Fira'. It is normally argued that it is derived from 'Thera', the ancient name of the island.

A Walk Around the Narrow Streets and the Museum

This view, however, runs into opposition from the linguists, who derive 'Fira' from the adjective pyrros meaning reddish, flame-coloured, or even yellowish, and which has come into modern Greek as fyrros or fyros, with the same meaning and is widely used in island placenames.

Fira is a long and narrow settlement with its main axis running north-south. It is built on the edge of the cliff and is encircled by two streets. The westerly one (Agiou Mina street and its extension M. Nomikou street) lies over the cliff, whilst to the east, Erythrou Stavrou street runs inland and has no view whatsoever. Between these two outer streets which frame the town is a third, central, one –the main axis of the town. This is Ypapantis street and is extended to the south by Mitropoleos street whilst to the north it is interrupted by the beginning of M. Nomikou street, which runs at right angles to it. Still further north, Agiou Ioannou street begins which could, from a certain viewpoint, be considered as the extension of the main street. As these three streets run north, they converge, finally coming together in Firostefani square. There are no cars in Fira. All the streets mentioned above are old, narrow and cobbled, with steps and sudden rises. Finally, east of the town is a fourth street. This is 25th Martiou street which, in reality, forms part of the main road axis

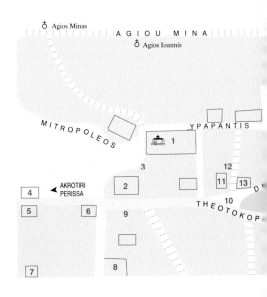

crossing the island from Oia to Perissa. Approximate half way through Fira, this street widens out and forms long narrow square, which is Theotokopoulou squa from where the buses and taxis start and which is forev bustling with people, traffic and motion. We shall take t

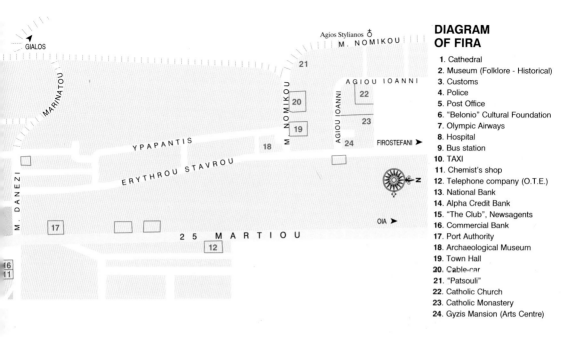

GIALOS

Agios Stylianos ☧
M. NOMIKOU

21

AGIOU IOANNI

22

23

24   FIROSTEFANI ▶

OIA ▶

MARINATOU

M. DANEZI

YPAPANTIS

18

19

20

M. NOMIKOU

AGIOU IOANNI

ERYTHROU STAVROU

17

25 MARTIOU

12

16
11

DIAGRAM OF FIRA

1. Cathedral
2. Museum (Folklore - Historical)
3. Customs
4. Police
5. Post Office
6. "Belonio" Cultural Foundation
7. Olympic Airways
8. Hospital
9. Bus station
10. TAXI
11. Chemist's shop
12. Telephone company (O.T.E.)
13. National Bank
14. Alpha Credit Bank
15. "The Club", Newsagents
16. Commercial Bank
17. Port Authority
18. Archaeological Museum
19. Town Hall
20. Cable-car
21. "Patsouli"
22. Catholic Church
23. Catholic Monastery
24. Gyzis Mansion (Arts Centre)

quare as the starting point for our routes around the
land and also as a reference point for the measurement
f distances (in kilometres). Only for our visit to Fira will we
tart from a different point –the intersection of Mich. Danezi
nd Ypapantis streets. In the northwest corner of Theoto-

kopoulou square, we find, and follow, Mich. Danezi street, which lies at right angles to the four parallel streets we have already mentioned, and we arrive at the point at which it cuts across Ypapantis street. This is the intersection which will be the starting point for our visit.

a) Fira - Southern Part

At the central junction of Fira is the impressive Belloneio Cultural Centre, painted ochre and cypress. It has a large hall for events with the most modern audiovisual equipment. It hosts musical, philological, theatrical and other events. Its library is remarkable and contains over 15,000 volumes.

We follow along Ypapantis street. There are shops on both sides of the street and the Theoxenia hotel on the left. After the hotel is a side road, also on the left, leading to the Theotokopoulou square. The buildings begin to thin out and there are considerable sections of the road with an uninterrupted view over the cliff. Continuing a little further, we meet a low wall, known locally as boundi, from where we can marvel at the landscape. This landscape is one of the most interesting elements of this route and is perhaps the most characteristic of the whole island. This is the view shown on most postcards, posters, book covers and advertisements.

The church of Agios Minas, on the tip of the rock to our left, has become something of a symbol of Santorini. Directly in front of us is a complex of blindingly white terraces, yards and steps; endless, completely white, leading down into the distance as they follow the slope of the cliff.

The last row of houses has the sea as a backdrop, which lies two hundred and fifty metres further down. To our left in the distance is Akrotiri, which extends like a long, slender snake to embrace the caldera. To our right in the distance is Thirassia, and in the middle of the caldera lies the volcano, like a huge black sleeping sea monster.

Majestic, impressive colours make their appearance at sunset.
1. Fira.
2. Ypapantis street.
3. Fira with a view towards the volcano.

Kato Fira

A few metres beyond the boundi is the start of a path winding downhill with broad steps, which will bring us closer to the houses and courtyards we saw from above. We enter the quarter which, by virtue of its position, is known as Kato Fira (Lower Fira). As we descend, we approach the church of Agios Yiannis on our right. Our elevated position enables us to examine from above its design, and we marvel at the variety and combination of the masses which go to make it up. The dome is supported on an octagonal drum with one window in each side.

It is very rarely that one is able to see the dome of a church from so close. The eight sides of the drum are of a dark-coloured and striking limestone, which sets them off and at the base of the cross there is a relief carved into the shape of a star which would be entirely pointless if the observer did not pass so close to the top of the dome.

After a turn, the road leads into the courtyard of the church and from there to Agiou Mina street which follows the edge of the cliff. We continue to the left, losing ourselves in the back-streets of Kato Fira –a different world, quiet and remote with a pace of its own only a few metres from the bustle and noise. We reach the church of Agios Minas, with its typically Santorinian dome composed of three elements, a) the polyhedral drum with one opening in each side, b) the dome itself with one or two rows of pro-truding stones which make it reminiscent of an explosive mine, and c) the turret on the top of the key stone of the dome, also consisting of a polyhedral drum with openings and supporting a second, smaller dome which bears the cross.

From here on, our road turns left and begins ciimbing uphill once more, bringing us back to the level of Ypapantis street, which we reach after passing in front of the third church on our route, that of Metamorphosi tou Sotiras (Transfig-uration of the Saviour), with its fine iron grates at the windows. We arrive at the top and enter Mitropoleos street, the continuation of Ypapantis street. We turn left (that is, in a northerly direction

The cathedral dominates the town.

and reach the point from which we began. Here we see the mansion of the Metropolitan. Continuing, we meet, on our left, the large Atlantis hotel, after which the road widens (as the beginning of Ypapantis street) and to our right rises the Orthodox cathedral of Santorini –the church of Ypapantis or Panagia tou Belonia. The original church was built in 1827 by M. Belonia and belonged to his family. In the early part of the 20th century, it was renovated and donated to the Municipality of Thera.

It was a magnificent building, painted ochre and with two tall bell-towers in its façade, to the right and left of the main entrance. It dominated the landscape of Fira. This building was completely destroyed in the earthquakes and in its place was erected another, completely different structure. Whilst the first church dominated by virtue of its height, the present building does so with its mass and width, a contribution also being made by the large courtyard and the colonnade. On the outside it is white, the windows and the colonnade being the only decoration. The interior, however, is decorated with many interesting hagiographs, the work of Christophoros Asimis, who also painted all the hagiographs in the church of Agios Charalambos at Exo Gonia.

Immediately after the Panagia tou Belonia, the road leads, right, to the post office and the banks.

Our walk is over, and we return to our starting point at Theotokopoulou square.

b) Fira - Northern Part

We start again from the intersection of Ypapantis and Danezi streets and follow the right branch of Ypapantis street which ascends with broad steps. To the right and left are shops mainly selling souvenirs. This street always had shops; it was a good commercial street of Fira with drapers, shoe shops, the Notary's office and newsagents. At the top of the road, standing at right angles to its axis, is The Leschi (The Club) with its marble entrance and carved pediment. In the old days, this building was used as a gambling club, from where it took its name. Later it was transformed into a kind of coffee shop with billiard tables. The inscription on the pediment of The Club informs us that it was built in 1871.

We continue along our road, which detours around The Club and follows the rise towards the north. At the point at which the road bypasses The Club, is a stairway to the right leading down into a parallel street where we find the market of Fira. It is worth spending some time in the alleyways near here, which are full of people, tourist shops, restaurants, coffee shops and bars.

To our left, the houses, built at a level quite a bit lower than the road, allow us to enjoy the view to the sea. As we ascend, we come to three interesting examples of the old mansion-houses of the island. The first is that of the Sarpakis family. The two wings of the house occupied the space to the right and left of the road. The left wing, of which we see the terrace, extended under the street and communicated with the right wing which was built higher. At no. 76 is the second mansion, that of the Nomikos family, with the same arrangement as the previous house in relation to the road. It is, however, more modern, having been built after the earthquakes on the site of two older buildings

Finally, the third mansion is that of the Vazengiou family, which stands at the top of M. Nomikou street. The main entrance of this house is exactly opposite Ypapantis street. The Vazengiou mansion was repaired after the earthquake and has reverted to its original form.

On the right-hand corner of Ypapantis and M. Nomikou streets is the Archaeological Museum, which stands on the site of the old National Bank.

After visiting the Museum, we take the short downhill stretch of M. Nomikou street (eastwards) reaching Erythrou Stavrou street and turning left (north). The picture presented by this street, as we see it from the spot at which we stand, with its barrel vaulting and the crossbeams which roof it at various points, is among the most charming spots on the island and a favourite subject for painters and photographers. At no. 182, on the right, is the marble entrance to another old mansion, that of the Koutsogiannopoulos family. On the pediment over the entrance are the initials of the first owner, Γ. Κ. Μ., and the date of construction, 1882.

1. Picturesque alleyway in the market of Fira.
2, 3. Panoramic view of Fira with the white houses, countless churches and the alleyways.

Directly opposite the entrance to this mansion, starts Agiou Ioannou street, climbing up at right angles to Erythrou Stavrou street. On the right-hand corner of Agiou Ioannou and Erythrou Stavrou streets, stands the Gyzis mansion.

The **Gyzis Mansion** (17th century) is one of the oldest buildings in Fira. Today it belongs to the Catholic bishopric, which has restored it and given it new uses to make it once more part of the life of the town. The mansion is used as an arts centre, with a hall suitable for events of all kinds and large exhibition rooms. We enter a white-painted internal courtyard surrounded by the tall wings of the building. The light is so strong on Santorini, and its reflection from the white walls so blinding, that it is nearly impossible to believe that one is in the shade. Note the distinctive decoration of the yard in the arches which surround it, carved from dark-coloured limestone in sharp contrast to the white-washed walls. On the western side of the courtyard, a door leads to the old cellar of the house, which has been converted into an events hall without destroying either the grape press (on the left as we enter) or the tanks.

The main entrance to the house, which today leads to the exhibition rooms, is on the north side of the courtyard.

The Gyzis mansion comes alive mainly in the summer thanks to the various events (theatrical performances, concerts and exhibitions) which take place there. Details of these events are only available on the spot.

Coming out of the Gyzis mansion, we leave Erythrou Stavrou street which continues northwards, deserted and lonely now, as far as Firostefani. For those who are fond of solitude, the walk from here to the square in Firostefani is marvellous. We shall follow Agiou Ioannou street, the main street of the Catholic quarter.

1. The entrance to the Gyzis mansion.
2. The courtyard of the Gyzis mansion.
3. The Domos bell-tower.
4. The church of Agios Ioannis tou Vaptisti.
5. The carpet-weaving factory in the convent of the Adelfon tou Eleous.

1

2

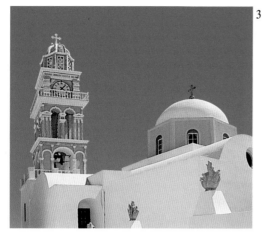

3

4

5

On our right, after the Gyzis mansion, is a raised area which gives access to two Catholic convents. On the left, once we are on this raised area, is the magnificent entrance to the **Convent of the Adelfon tou Eleous** (Sisters of Mercy), who settled on Santorini in 1841. The convent once had a school, a hospital and a dispensary run by the nuns, but all this came to an end with the earthquakes at which time the nuns left the island. Today, most of the convent has been restored and houses the offices of the Catholic see, a hostel for organized groups of young people from abroad and a very interesting carpet-weaving workshop where many girls from the island learn this difficult and tiring art. The convent and the factory can be visited during working hours. At the far side of the raised area, is the entrance to the Convent of the Dominikanidon (Dominican Nuns), a small but exquisite building with a balustrade. Dominican nuns, it will be remembered, live in complete retreat and for this reason the convent is not open to visitors. To its right, however, is its church, the Rozaria, which is open to visitors and is well worth seeing as a fine example of the combination of the island's style and Baroque.

We return to Agiou Ioannou street. On our right rises the bell-tower of the Domos, the **church of Agios Ioannis tou Vaptisti** (the Baptist), the Catholic cathedral. This church was severely damaged by the earthquake and, although it has been restored, much of the Baroque element in its interior decoration has not been renewed.

We continue with the Convent of the Sisters of Mercy on our right. The road is covered by enormous arches at a number of points and soon turns right running directly north. Now it is more or less an extension of Ypapantis street, which was interrupted by the Vazengiou mansion and the Domos which stands directly behind it. We can go only a little further before coming to a narrow roadway with steps leading to the edge of the cliff. To our right at this point is the entrance to the island's third Catholic monastery, that of the Lazariston (Lazarists), and also the entrance to its monastery church.

We walk down the narrow road with the steps and are back in M. Nomikou street. Before turning left to come to Ypapantis and Danezi streets, it is worth taking a couple of steps to the right to see the church of **Agios Stylianos**, a Lilliputian chapel which seems to cling desperately to the edge of the cliff for fear of sliding off and smashing. The road continues north to the 'Frangika' quarter and from there to Firostefani.

Going down M. Nomikou street to the point at which it turns left, we reach the turning known as **Patsouli**. This turning has something very charming about it; for many people it is the most beautiful spot on the island – it is certainly the most romantic. It offers an incomparable view down over the road to Gialos, Limanaki and Trypes and, for those who seek it, the memory of the festivities of the past: groups of merry-makers making their way up on foot from Gialos, whilst others would be waiting for them at the top, at Patsouli, and all together would be singing with great humour and stamina.

One can spend hours at Patsouli just waiting for the sun to set. In any case, our walk is over.

A little further along to the left is the entrance to the cable-car and immediately after that, the Vazengiou mansion.

View of Fira from Patsouli.
The chapel of Agios Stylianos.

Archaeological Museum

The archaeological museum of Fira hosts mainly finds from the excavations at Mesa Vouno conducted by **Friedrich Hiller von Gaertringen** between 1896 and 1900. There are also finds and private collections from previous digs and some from more recent excavations of the Akrotiri site led by archaeologist **Spyros Marinatos** (see Archaeological Sites, page 68).

Among the more important exhibits the visitor can see are:
– Marble figurines dating from the 3rd millennium BC.
– Female statuettes of a devotional nature.
– Marble kouroi.
– Examples of reliefs and statues from Hellenistic and Roman times.
– Archaic vessels from Mesa Vouno, mostly kylixes with painted representations of triremes and horses.
– Skyphos cups from Akrotiri.
– Pithoi from Mesa Vouno and Akrotiri.
   (Many important finds from the excavations at Akrotiri have been moved and are housed in the Archaeological Museum of Athens).

1. Inside the museum of Santorini.
2. Statue of Aphrodite, a sample of Theran plastic arts (Archaeological Museum of Fira).
3. The head of a large kouros with the characteristic hairstyle of the Deadalic art (7th century BC).
4. Large pithos with relief decoration of the Archaic period. On the upper part is depicted a swan and below this, winged horses pulling chariots.
5. Geometric krater (Museum of Thera).

ARCHAEOLOGICAL SITES

Akrotiri - Ancient Thera

From Fira, we follow the road to Perissa and after about ten kilometres we turn left to Akrotiri. Fourteen and a half kilometres from Fira, on our left before the beach, is the entrance to the ancient site.

The excavations at Akrotiri were begun in 1967 by the archaeologist Sp. Marinatos and their aim was to prove the theory that the cause of the destruction of the Minoan civilization in Crete was the eruption of the volcano on Santorini

Results from the excavations were most revealing. An entire Minoan town with two- and three-storey houses decorated with wonderful murals of the style found in the Minoan palaces of Crete, the most important being the 'Flotilla', the 'Spring Fresco' and the 'Boxing Children'. There were also a number of pots, pitharia, bronze vessels and furniture found in the houses. Apart from confirming the above-mentioned theory, the results from the excavations led archaeologists to draw the following conclusions:

a) The eruption of the volcano was preceded by earthquakes and the inhabitants had plenty of time to get organized and abandon their

The excavation uncovered an entire town with exceptional wall-paintings.

dwellings (no skeletons, neither human nor animal, were found. Nor were any objects of value).

b) There may have been a period of calm which allowed some of the inhabitants to return and try to repair their half-ruined houses (tools have been found thrown down at various points), they too, however, had time to leave.

c) The period of time between earthquakes and eruption may have been as much as a year (seeds had time to sprout before being covered by lava).

d) Akrotiri was the site of an organized community with a high standard of living, possibly governed by an order of priests.

e) Nature and fertility were the objects of religious worship.

f) Each house had a special place of worship, skilfully decorated predominantly with murals but there were no temples.

g) The art of the inhabitants of Akrotiri had similarities to Cretan art of the Minoan period.

h) No written records were found to allow archaeologists to draw clearer conclusions, but there are indications to support the identification of Strongyle with Atlantis.

The Excavation Site

We enter the site which is one of a unique nature. Most of the archaeological sites we know (the Acropolis at Athens, Delphi, Olympia, Pella, Dodona, Epidaurus, Mycenae and Knossos) are monuments. They belong to no one. One marvels at their beauty, their splendour and technical perfection, but one's admiration remains outside the life of which they were a part because all these monuments were connected with special moments or aspects of this life, which in turn were directly linked to the civilizations which created them. For the few who have studied those civilizations, the monuments become articulate and sometimes even verbose witnesses. Perhaps these people can bring the monuments back to life by an effort of the imagination. For many, however, the monuments remain mute.

On the other hand, the area we are now entering is a familiar one; a place for daily life and routine. There are two- and three-storey houses, doors, windows, toilets, kitchens, workshops, lanes, drains and shops. All this belongs, or belonged, to people one can easily imagine living there because one can easily imagine oneself living among them. One may even feel as though one were trespassing when entering other people's houses just because the owners have run away and left them. And when, inevitably, one thinks that these houses were built 3,500 years ago, one will be astonished because all the time expressed in that enormous number seems in no way to intrude between us and the houses.

The excavations have uncovered a long and narrow section of the town running north-south (see plan of the ancient town, next page), with the entrance on the south side.

We enter and head north. On our left, the first large building we come to under the protective roof, Xeste 3, has been named from its façade of cut stone (xeste = ashlar). The ground floor consists of approximately ten rooms. An impressive staircase leads to the first floor and there are indications that there was a second floor as well. In this house were found wall paintings which, altogether, cover a total surface area of approximately 100 m².

We continue north entering the stone paved Telchines Street, To our left is Building Γ. To our right, the two-storey Building B, in which were found the following wall-paintings: the 'Antelopes', the 'Boxing Children' and the 'Blue Monkeys'.
The basement of B1 was a storeroom in which pithoi were found in special niches in the walls.

We continue along the right (east) side of town, leaving Building Γ for the return journey. The road widens to form Mill Square, a name derived from the small rooms which are to be seen on its northern side and which were the workshop of a miller. The mill for grinding the wheat can still be seen inside, as can the built-in pithari into which the flour fell.

The mill is the northwest extremity (Δ15) of Complex Δ which spreads out on our right as we continue. The western entrance to this complex, under the propylon, leads to the following areas:

1. Jars on the site.
2. Part of the ruins: room 22 on the eastern side of sector Δ.
Previous Page: The rocky landscape with the lilies and the swallows that fly around in daring formations.
(National Archaeological Museum).

Δ1: The ground floor of this area, to judge from the utensils and fittings, must have been a kitchen. The upper floor shows a typical characteristic of Minoan architecture: it was divided in two by a series of doors which supported the roof.

Δ2: Contained the 'Spring' wall-painting –a landscape with lilies among which swallows frolic.

Δ9: A huge number of pots were found here, as also in Δ16 where they were arranged according to size, shape and quality. Δ16, therefore, was probably a shop.

The external wall of Δ1 and the house opposite it (the West House or House of the Fishermen) form the Triangular Square. We cross this and head north.

There is another entrance to Complex Δ on its northern side, behind which a staircase leads to the upper floor.

We continue to the northernmost part of the site, where we find Building A, which must have been a storehouse. This at least is the conclusion to be drawn from the vast number of pithoi uncovered there. In some of these jars, carbonized remains of flour, barely and other foodstuffs were found. Building A also produced part of a wall-painting whose subject (the head of an African with curly hair, an earring and thick lips), has not been encountered anywhere else in Minoan Cretan art. This building is the first which came to light during excavations. After Building A, we turn south once more to visit the western part of the town.

First we come, on the right, to the House of the Ladies, in which were found murals showing bare-breasted ladies, as in Crete, and others representing papyri. Apart from pottery, stone tools were also found in this house. We return to the Triangular Square and in its northwestern corner we see the House of the Fishermen in which were found two murals showing fishermen, one with a priestess and the famous mural with the ships.

We continue south reaching Mill Square again and enter Telchines Street

On our right is Building Γ in which many stone tools were found.

AKROTIRI: A Civilization Buried Beneath the Ash

Now that you have completed your tour around the excavation site, find a quiet corner, close your eyes and let the Cycladic light that illuminated these narrow streets for 3,500 years, pass through you and recall the vivid images of the past. Immediately, the playful screams of the children reach your ears as they run from the coast up to the little squares of the settlement, the clamour of the market and the yelling of the merchants.

Nature generously endows this place with its goodness. The people live peacefully, and respect nature and the good things of life. Merchants, seamen, farmers, craftsmen and artists all enjoy a high standard of living which we see in every aspect of their daily life. It is a society with profound urban characteristics which continuously expands its horizons because of the external trade links which bring it into daily contact with the various cultures developed by the peoples of the eastern Mediterranean.

This area is seismically active and that is why the skilled master craftsmen used wood to strengthen the stone constructions. They inserted joists to support the roofs, floors and the walls, and the interior doors are surrounded by wooden frames so that the construction will better stand the anger of the earthquakes. The floor at ground level is usually covered with trampled earth. If we go up to the upper floor, however, we will see large windows that provide air and light and the floor here is covered with schist slabs or a mosaic made of trampled earth, pebbles and broken shells.

Also here on the upper floor, on the walls of the rooms, the Theran artist creates the identity of the island's people with pictures, so that future generations will find it.

The artist depicts the beauty of the nature and the love of the people, giving life and

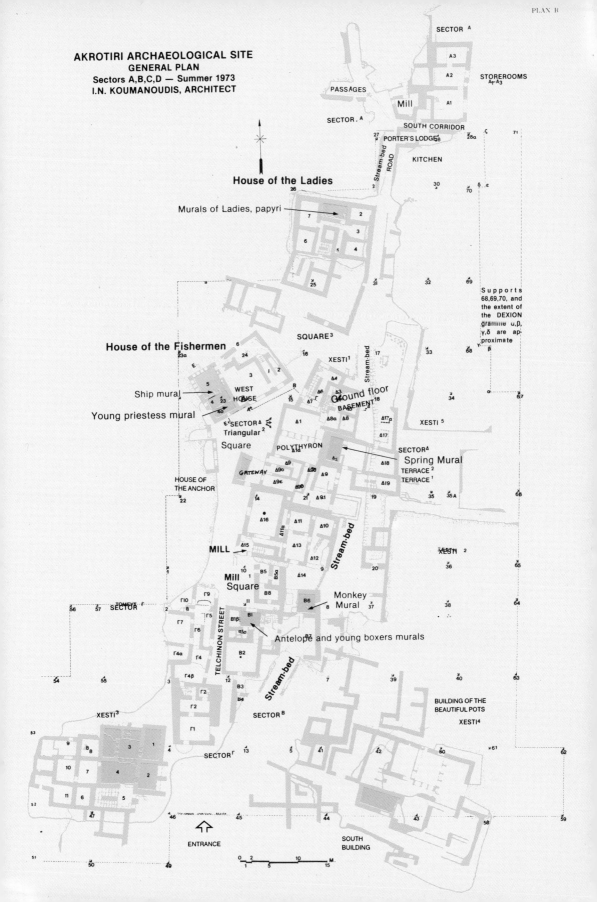

AKROTIRI ARCHAEOLOGICAL SITE
GENERAL PLAN
Sectors A,B,C,D — Summer 1973
I.N. KOUMANOUDIS, ARCHITECT

SECTOR A

A3

A2

STOREROOMS
A₂ A₃

A1

Mill

PASSAGES

SECTOR. A

SOUTH CORRIDOR

PORTER'S LODGE

ROAD

KITCHEN

House of the Ladies

Murals of Ladies, papyri

Supports 68,69,70, and the extent of the DEXION gramme α,β, γ,δ are approximate

SQUARE³

House of the Fishermen

XESTI¹

Stream-bed

Ground floor
BASEMENT

XESTI⁵

Ship mural

WEST HOUSE

Young priestess mural

SECTOR
Triangular Square

SECTOR
Spring Mural
TERRACE²
TERRACE¹

POLYTHYRON

HOUSE OF THE ANCHOR

GATEWAY

MILL

XESTI²

Mill Square

Stream-bed

Monkey Mural

SECTOR
TOMBS

TELCHINON STREET

Antelope and young boxers murals

XESTI³

Stream-bed

SECTOR ᴮ

BUILDING OF THE BEAUTIFUL POTS

XESTI⁴

SECTOR ᴳ

ENTRANCE

SOUTH BUILDING

0 2   10   M.
1   5   20

Fisherman holding a bunch of fish, from Room 5 of the west house.

An adult woman shows a young girl how to collect flowers of the plant known since antiquity for its use as a spice, colouring, aromatic but also as a medicine. The lily collectors come from Room 3 of the first floor of Xeste 3.

motion to the plants, birds and animals and giving us the feeling of a tasteful, sensitive, sensible people. He flies above the plains and the sea and his pictures are a hymn to the joy of life. With the azure, black, yellow and red, he gives life to the flat walls. Lilies and crocuses, cypresses and pine trees and even the juices of the bunches of grapes which the greedy Cycladic sun devours. He fills out the sails of the grand sailing vessels which travel to Crete for alabaster and clay, to Cyprus for copper and to Syria for gypsum and porphyry, returning then to the sweet embrace of their homeland.

The artist wants the people to be beautiful and happy. The women have pale bodies shown dynamic and free. They wear pretty dresses, decorated with jewellery and ribbons. The men have dark bodies and are dressed according to their professions. The captains wear a broad sleeveless cloak, the youths wear short skirts, as do the sailors, whilst the soldiers sport helmets made of wild boars' tusks and hold large rectangular shields made of hide.

In the houses we find many ceramics of a decorative or functional nature. Here we witness the unbreakable bond between daily life, art and high-level aesthetics. Luxurious homemade pots, elaborate cookware, show the unusual aesthetic conception and the high standard of the art of cooking. The pictures that decorate the ceramics are various. We see linear motifs, pictures from the plant and animal kingdoms: lilies, grapes, crocuses, myrtles, birds, wild goats, but also dolphins which, of the animals, are the most favoured topic for the Theran artist.

The household is completed by the loom which we find in the upper rooms. The unequal weights stretch the woolen or linen cloth which is used for making clothes, covers or sails for the ships.

A great civilization flourished here and left behind for all of us, elements of an ancient mosaic buried beneath the ashes which make up the picture which the visitor will enclose within his soul when he leaves.

ANCIENT THERA
(1115 - 630 BC)

The Phoenicians who, according to mythology settled on the island in the 14th century BC, gave it the name Calliste. At the end of the 12th century BC, the Dorians, under King Theras, changed the name of the island and gave it the name of their king. During this period, from around 1115 BC up to 630 BC, ports, towns and sanctuaries were built (see section on Myths and History). Later, during the Hellenistic period, the island was a naval base for the Ptolemies and ancient Thera, which we shall visit, dates from this time.

Our visit begins from the northwestern edge and we will continue southeast. The excavations of the area were, as we have already mentioned in the museum of Fira, led by Baron von Gaertringen between 1896 and 1900. The finds prove that Dorian colonists inhabited the area already by the 9th century BC and that during the Hellenistic period the Ptolemies (300 - 145 BC) had a strong garrison here, directly above the island's port –ancient Oia (today Kamari). In other words, in the 4th century BC, Kamari and Mesa Vouno were an Egyptian naval base. As well as these, there are also Byzantine remains at Mesa Vouno.

1. Wall painting from the House of the Ladies (National Archaeological Museum of Athens).
2. Ancient Thera today.

2

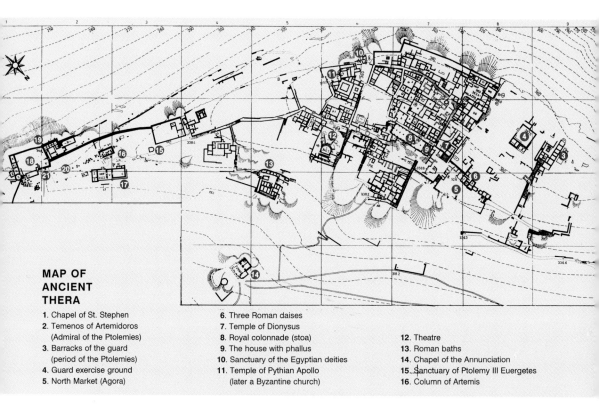

**MAP OF
ANCIENT
THERA**

1. Chapel of St. Stephen
2. Temenos of Artemidoros
   (Admiral of the Ptolemies)
3. Barracks of the guard
   (period of the Ptolemies)
4. Guard exercise ground
5. North Market (Agora)

6. Three Roman daises
7. Temple of Dionysus
8. Royal colonnade (stoa)
9. The house with phallus
10. Sanctuary of the Egyptian deities
11. Temple of Pythian Apollo
    (later a Byzantine church)

12. Theatre
13. Roman baths
14. Chapel of the Annunciation
15. Sanctuary of Ptolemy III Euergetes
16. Column of Artemis

The first remains we shall encounter on entering the archaeological site are Byzantine. They lie beneath the chapel of Agios Stefanos, and are of a 4th or 5th century basilica dedicated to the Archangel Michael. We continue along the path and after about two hundred metres we come, on our left, to the temenos of Artemidorus, the admiral of the Ptolemies, with inscriptions, the symbols of various gods (Zeus, Apollo and Poseidon) and dedications to others (Priapus and Hecate among them).

A hundred metres or so further on, to the right, a stepped path climbs up to the barracks of the garrison of the Ptolemies. To the left of the barracks was the gymnasium of the garrison. We continue along the main path, which a little further on widens out to the left and becomes the **agora** (111 m long by 17 - 30 m wide). We are at its north end and as we walk along, we shall see three Roman exedras. Immediately after these, on the right again, we reach the temple of Dionysus, to which a series of steps lead. Now we are in the central portion of the agora, and we

walk towards the southern part which, on its left on the downward slope, has a group of houses and on its right the Royal Stoa (41.5 m x 10.1 m) with a colonnade along its main axis.
Immediately in front of the stoa is the house with the phallus and the inscription "*ΤΟΙΣ ΦΙΛΟΙΣ*" (to my friends). Behind the stoa and slightly higher, is a large group of houses.

The Sacred Way begins in the southern corner of the agora and leads south. As soon as we enter upon it, we have, on our right, a large rectangular open area. A little beyond the southwest corner of this open area, was the **sanctuary of Isis, Serapis and Anubis**, and to the left of this was **the temple of Pythian Apollo** on which a Byzantine church was later built.

We continue along the Sacred Way. To our left is the **theatre**, as converted by the Romans, with the **baths** (also from the Roman period) behind it and a little to the south. Even further over, on the downward slope, we can see the chapel of Evangelismou tou Theotokou (the Annunciation of the Virgin).

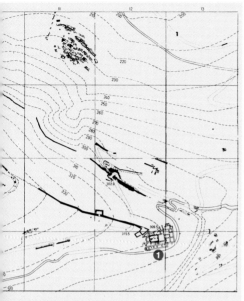

17. Temple of Carneian Apollo
18. Training-ground of the ephebes
19. Baths of the ephebes
20. Terrace of the dancing
21. Cave of Hermes and Heracles

After a short while, the Sacred Way disappears and becomes a path once more, following which, we come, in sequence, to the **sanctuary of Ptolemy III Euergetes, the Stele of Artemis, the temple of Apollo Karneios** and, finally, the **Gymnasium of the Ephebes** with baths and a training ground. To the left of the gymnasium is **the cave of Hermes and Heracles**. This is where our visit to the archaeological site ends, and we can now return to Kamari for a swim and a meal.

1. Remains from the Hellenistic period on ancient Thera.
2. The Royal Stoa, the centre of public life, built in the era of Augustus.
3, 4. Reliefs at the temenos of Artemidorus.

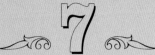

ROUTES AROUND THE ISLAND

After the walk around the majestic capital of the island, we will, beginning with Fira, visit the small picturesque villages which each add their own character to the uniqueness of the landscape.

Whichever route you choose, and by whatever means of transport you travel, you are certain not to be disappointed. By car, boat or donkey you will be fascinated by the domed churches and the imposing castles, the white-washed houses and the dazzlingly white yards. It is, however, recommended that you not restrict yourself to the organized tours which include only the famous sites. Choose one or more of the routes from the seven we suggest below and explore the island; discover its hidden beauties.

Route 1: *Fira - Oia*

Route 2: *Monolithos - Airport*

Route 3: *Pyrgos - Profitis Ilias*

Route 4: *Kamari - Mesa Vouno*

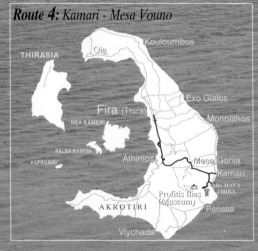

Route 1

Fira - Oia (16 km)

**Fira - Firostefani - Agios Nikolaos Nunnery
Imerovigli - Finikia - Perivolos - Oia**

Return via the northeast coast:

**Tholos - Baxedes - Koloumbos
Panagia tou Kalou - Vourvoulos
Kontochori - Fira**

The main interest of this route is that it includes all the villages built on the rim of the cliff and which look down into the caldera: Firostefani, Imerovigli and Oia.

During the route, the visitor will become familiar with the volcanic nature of the island –its most notable feature– and will enjoy, from a number of different angles, a unique view. He may also swim in the waters of the caldera which can be reached at the bays of Ammoudi and Armeni, or on the east side of Oia at the Baxedes and Koloumbos beaches.

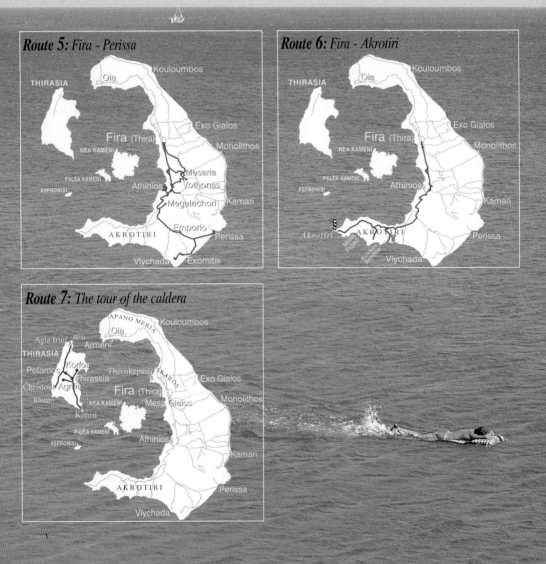

Route 5: *Fira - Perissa*

THIRASIA · Oia · Kouloumbos · Exo Gialos · Fira (Thira) · NEA KAMENI · Monolithos · PALEA KAMENI · Mesaria · ASPRONISI · Athinios · Vothonas · Megalochori · Kamari · Emporio · AKROTIRI · Perissa · Vlychada · Exomitis

Route 6: *Fira - Akrotiri*

THIRASIA · Oia · Kouloumbos · Exo Gialos · Fira (Thira) · NEA KAMENI · Monolithos · PALEA KAMENI · ASPRONISI · Athinios · Akrotiri · AKROTIRI · Mesa Pigadi · Kokkini Ammos · Kamari · Perissa · Vlychada

Route 7: *The tour of the caldera*

APANO MERIA · Kouloumbos · Agia Irini · Riva · Oia · Armeni · THIRASIA · Kortos · Theoskepasti · SKAROS · Exo Gialos · Potamos · Thirassia · Fira (Thira) · Christos · Agria · Monolithos · Kinimo · NEA KAMENI · Mesa Gialos · Kimisi · PALEA KAMENI · ASPRONISI · Athinios · Kamari · AKROTIRI · Perissa · Vlychada

Firostefani

From the square of Fira, we take the road which heads towards the northern part of the island. The settlement of Fira stretches out to our left and merges with the village of Firostefani, the square of which we reach after a distance of 800 metres. It is claimed by some, that the name of the village used to be Firon Stefani (Crown of Fira). Firostefani is an extension of Fira and, on a different scale, could be thought of as the northern suburbs of the capital. It is an elongated little village, built on the edge of the cliff, with a square, restaurants, hotels, coffee-shops and the impressive church of Agios Gerasimos, which –unusually for the island– is surrounded by tall cypresses. Firostefani offers a marvellous view of the caldera, different to that from Fira, and the cliff here is much steeper. To the right we look out over the island's most elegant and majestic rock mass, Skaros. The volcano has changed shape: already visible, behind and to the right, is the long, narrow mass of Palia Kameni, parallel to the sea. Walking north from the square, we enter the main part of the village. To the left we see the ruins of two old windmills. Further along and also on the left, are two lanes leading to the sloping part of the village, built on the side of the cliff. This part of the village has been almost completely restored and there is an especially fine variety of shapes, masses and colours created by the courtyards, the flat roofs and protruding parts of the skafta houses, which we see from above. The road leading south from the square along the edge of the cliff leads to Fira. After about fifty metres, we see the Catholic church of Firostefani, Panagia ton Agion Theodoron, which celebrates on the 15th of August. Immediately after the church, and up to Fira, the area with the amazing view is inhabited mainly by Catholics and is known as **Frangika** (see also page 62).

Continuing to the northern part of the island, after Firostefani we reach the nunnery of Agios Nikolaos which was founded in 1651 by the Gyzis family, one of the few Orthodox families living at that time in the Skaros fortress. The nunnery was originally located on Skaros where it operated normally until 1815.

However, when the settlement was abandoned, the nuns decided to move and found a new establishment in a more accessible location and they chose the site

where we see it today. The new nunnery was built, after many attempts, between 1819 and 1821, was coenobite and had forty cells. The katholikon has three parts: one of its chapels is dedicated to Agios Panteleimonas and the other to Zoodochos Pigi, whilst the central one is dedicated to Agios Nikolaos. Note the fine wooden iconostasis in the katholikon and the Byzantine icon of Agios Nikolaos. The main occupation of the nuns was weaving and they also devoted a considerable amount of time to the maintenance, care and cleanliness of the nunnery which, from this point of view, continues to be impressive.

Magical view from Firostefani.
Thirassia is visible in the distance.

Imerovigli - Skaros

After the nunnery of Agios Nikolaos, and only two kilometres from Fira, is Imerovigli. The name presumably comes from the days of piracy, and means 'the day-time lookout post'. The site of the village, more or less in the centre of the caldera and at its highest point, would certainly have made it possible to keep watch over the whole area and give a timely warning to the islanders should pirates appear.

It is a wonderful village that combines the harmony and quietness which are difficult to find in other areas of Santorini. It is built on the most favourable site of the Theran caldera, looking towards the volcano with Thirassia visible in the distance. The church of Imerovigli, Panagia the Malteza, takes its name from the icon around which it centres and which was found in the sea near Malta. As we pass through the village in the direction of the caldera, we come across the path to Skaros. Formerly one of the five most important settlements on the island, very few traces of the town now remain.

One of the most exciting walks the island has to offer, which takes at least one hour, is that which leads, on Skaros, along the path which runs to the Theoskepasti chapel. This dazzlingly white, towering chapel is embedded in the rocks, and commands the abyss from above. We stand, here, at the most majestic point of the island; the view and the feeling of awe emitted by the landscape are sensational. From the square of Imerovigli, we continue along the same road as before towards Oia.

At a distance of 2.3 kilometres, is a road to the right which leads to the village of Vourvoulos, through which we shall pass on the way back.

Further down the road and on the left, we see the Imerovigli cemetery.

Reaching 3.6 kilometres, we see, to the left, the start of the small path which gives a view over the caldera and the settlement of Oia.

From this point on, and until the ninth kilometre, we shall meet, to the right and left of the road, a number of paths and lanes of no particular interest.

Finikia - Perivolos

Nine kilometres from the centre of Fira, to the right of the road is the village of Finikia which, together with Perivolos and Oia, make up the island's most northerly inhabited complex, known as Apano Meria (Upper Part). At ten kilometres, a road to the left leads to Perivolos. It is one of the most beautiful beaches of Santorini which, in recent years, has seen a substantial rise in tourism. Major hotel complexes, as well as bars on the beach, have significantly increased the amount of traffic, especially during the day. A junction follows, the right branch of which leads to Finikia; a small settlement known for the hospitality of its inhabitants, the picturesque lanes and its traditional tavernas. After Perivolos, the road leading to the northeast coast of the island begins. This is the road we shall be taking on our return to Fira.

1. The majestic rock of Skaros.
2. The settlement of Finikia.
Previous page: Panoramic view from Firostefani.

Imerovigli with Oia in the background.

Oia

Oia, the name is very ancient, is eleven kilometres from Fira and overlooks the northwest side of the island, welcoming its visitors with a unique combination of colours and a magical landscape. During the period of Frankish Occupation, Oia was among the five largest settlements on the island. After liberation from the Turks, the inhabitants of Apano Meria became prominent seafarers. As they grew richer, they invested their money in large mansions. It is one of the few Cycladic villages which, despite its development in tourism, has managed to keep its traditional colour.

Its peculiar architecture provokes the admiration of all visitors. Houses are dug into the lava from the eruptions of the volcano, most of them two-storey. They give the village a special character of its own, not least because they are all painted. The walls are ochre and the door and window frames are red limestone. Even the central roads of Oia are pebbled with marble plaques instead of the cobbled roads we meet on the rest of the island.

Parallel with the **astonishing sunset** and the view of the volcano or the sea, the picturesque shops and flowered yards create a special harmony that charms even the most difficult visitor. The beauty of the place is also verified by the intricate coastlines that surround Oia.

There are two paths with steps, one running down the cliff to Armeni beach with its little chapel of Agios Nikolas on the rock, and the other going to Ammoudi beach. On the coast of Armeni, the visitor can enjoy his swim or go skiing, and he can taste fresh fish in the small tavernas. From the bay of Ammoudi there is a service to Thirassia, should one wish to visit this little island. The beach is ideal for swimming and romantic walks with the view of the sunset.

Before you end your tour of Oia, we suggest you visit the various galleries with works of modern art, items of folklore and traditional handicraft. Among other remains of Oia's past is its interesting maritime museum, preserving memories of the glories of the past. Rare figure heads, models of older and more recent ships which belonged to seamen of Santorini, water-colours of old sailing ships and photographic material and a library, all record, year after year, the contribution of the Therans to the glorious history of the Greek shipping.

Oia is one of the most beautiful villages and it charms you. It makes you feel more inclined to poetry and romanticism.

1. Inside the nautical museum.
2. The beach of Ammoudi, with the colours of the night.
3. From the castle of Oia the view is breathtaking.
4. The little beach opposite Ammoudi,
ideal for those who seek isolation.

Returning to Fira

(Tholos - Baxedes - Koloumbos
Panagia tou Kalou - Vourvoulos
Kontochori - Fira)

The Road starts at the intersection we have already noted at eleven kilometres and leads east. At twelve kilometres, to the left is the settlement called **Tholos**, a little village outside of Oia.

The road turns right, to the south, and follows the east coast of the island.

Fourteen kilometres along sees us at the region of **Baxedes**, an area with a sandy beach and rocks but which is undeveloped. At the seventeenth kilometre we are now on a height, the peak of a cape known as **Koloumbos**. It is a secluded sandy beach under Akrotiri.

On the east of the beach is the underwater volcano of Kouloumbos. In the sea nearby, at a depth of 18.5 metres, is the crater of the second volcano of Santorini –the one which erupted in AD 1650 (see page 18).

1. The beaches of the island are ideal not only for swimming but also for water sports.
2. The beach of Koloumbos.
3. The folklore museum in Kontochori.

After Koloumbos, there is a turning to the right which leads to the church of **Agios Giorgis the Xechoristi** (the Distinguished) which, according to the locals, is an offering from a believer to Agios Giorgis who helped him pay his debts. Further on, to the left are lanes leading to the coast.

Eighteen kilometres from Fira brings us to a turning on the right which leads to the area of Pori and the large church of **Panagia tou Kalou**. Panagia was built for the time of the bad eruption in 1650.

After the crossroads to Imerovigli there follows, on the right the church of Agios Artemios and on the left the church of Agia Irini.

At the 22 km stage, we meet a crossroads, the road left leads to Vourvoulos beach. We shall bear right for the village of **Vourvoulos**. It is a picturesque, non-tourist village whose inhabitants are involved in farming.

We follow the road through the village and turn south.

At 24 km, the left hand branch of the junction leads to the Kontochori beach, Apocho Gialos or Pigadia (meaning 'wells'). There are real wells here but the water is salty. There are also ruins of a tomato factory. We turn right and a little further on reach **Kontochori** –the eastern settlement of Fira. It lies in a hollow off the main road and for this reason is easy to pass by without noticing.

There are, however, two large mansions in it: those of the Dargentas and Kovaios families. Important here is the folklore museum of Em. Lignos on the road which is parallel to the central asphalt road, the undercut Theran house, the winery, the cave, the workshops (carpenter's, cooper's etc.), the gallery with works on the subject of Santorini by famous artists, an archive (with lithographs, books and manuscripts) and the chapel of Agios Konstantinos, which remind us of the life of the old inhabitants of the island.

After about 500 metres, we come to the square if Fira where our first route ends.

3

Route 2

Monolithos - Airport (21 km.)

Fira - Monolithos (harbour)
Fira - Airport

The purpose of this route, apart from a tour of the area, is largely to go swimming. Besides, the beach at Monolithos is the most suitable on the island for small children.

From Fira, we take the road leading to the southern part of the island and continue as far as the Messaria crossroads (3.4 km) where we turn left.

The crossroads that we meet leading to Kamari, we pass by.

Further on is a turning left which leads to Monolithos along a narrow road without passing the airport. There is no particular reason to go this way unless we are in a hurry.

The road continues straight ahead for a further 300 metres before ending at the airport. We follow the left branch of the road.

We are now seven kilometres along our route and our road ends at a three way crossroads. Directly in front of us rises the rock of Monolithos –from which the region gets its name– with the white chapel of Agios Yiannis in a niche. **Monolithos** is another remnant of Aegeis, like Mesa Vouno at Perissa, which means that before the volcano erupted for the first time it must have been a reef encircled by the sea. It is one of the most remarkable places of the island, with an organized beach of the characteristic black sand of Santorini and very clear waters.

We take the left branch of the three-way crossroads and after 700 metres reach the beach named **Limani** (harbour). In the past this name was used to describe the whole area, but today it has taken the name Monolithos. The two quays which enclose it explain the name and are evidence of efforts at some time to build the port of Santorini here. However, the location is entirely unsuitable for this because it is exposed to the winds and the seabed is shallow and sandy.

Thus the site was never used as a port. On the other hand, the beach provides excellent swimming, particularly for those who are not strong swimmers, since there is fine black sand and the water is shallow until quite a long way out.

To our left we see an abandoned tomato processing factory.

Further down is another tomato factory, this time belonging to the Co-operative, which is still in operation. Its products (tomato purée, tinned tomatoes and tomato juice) are of incomparable taste precisely because of the quality of the raw materials, and can be bought from the Co-operative's shop in Fira.

At 8.4 km, our route comes to the end of the road. From here on, there is only a sandy expanse along the beach which it would be unwise to attempt by car. Walking along it will eventually bring us to Exo Gialos tou Karteradou.

We return to the three-way crossroads at Monolithos, from which we take the branch which leads south. This road runs parallel to the airport runway, between it and the sea.

To the left, tracks run down to the sea, whilst to the right is the chapel of Agia Paraskevi within the airport perimeter.

At 9.1 km, we again reach the end of the road and of the route. A little further on in front of us, are the ruins of yet another tomato factory. Beyond this, Kamari beach begins but this is reached by another road.

1. Exo Gonia and high up the village of Pyrgos.
2. Monolithos with the white chapel of Agios Yiannis.

Route 3

Pyrgos - Profitis Ilias

Fira - Pyrgos - Exo Gonia - Profitis Ilias

Pyrgos is 2.2 km from Fira by the main Fira-Perissa road, and 9.4 km by the route described here. The visit to Exo Gonia adds four kilometres to the total.

To get from Fira to Pyrgos, it is possible to follow the Perissa road as far as the 6.8 km stage of the route. However, we suggest another route, a part of which (3 km) follows a fairly smooth track, which is shorter and has other points of interest. It is the old road which the muleteers used when going to Pyrgos with their animals. It is more or less straight and today serves the pumice quarries.

After 650 metres there is a turning to the right for the quarries, which the inhabitants of Santorini call Droumbes or Balades. They can be seen best from the sea, either on one's journey in by ship (in which case one passes in front of them before docking at Athinios), or on one's way to the volcano by boat.

Three kilometres along our way, we meet the Fira-Perissa road and follow it in the direction of Perissa. We are now 5.7 km along this road. We follow the turning left towards Pyrgos and turn left again for Exo Gonia.

Exo Gonia is a small settlement clinging to the side of the mountain and two kilometres from the main road. The size of the Agios Charalambos church is out of all proportion to the size of the village which it dominates from on high and it can be seen from almost every point on the island. The interior of the church is entirely covered with murals, the work of Christophoros Asimis. This road continues southeast passing through Mesa Gonia (Episkopi, see page 102) and finally joins the Kamari road.

We return to the main road and enter the village of Pyrgos (8 km).

Pyrgos

Pyrgos is the village which most vividly maintains the characteristics of the old Medieval settlements of Santorini, of which there were once four more on the island: Oia, Skaros, Emboreio and Akrotiri. Built on a hilltop far from the sea, Pyrgos was surrounded by a wall whose ruins can still be seen in the village. At a later date, the dangers of the Middle Ages vanished and houses began to be built outside the walls causing the village to take the shape it has today. Apart from its ruins, the old castle also survives in the name of the village which means 'tower' or 'castle'. Pyrgos has an incredible number of churches, some of which are quite old. The oldest of all is that of Kimissi tis Theotokos (the Dormition of the Virgin), or 'Theotokaki' (Little Virgin), in the castle of Pyrgos, which was

Above: Built on a height, Pyrgos vividly maintains the characteristics of its Medieval settlement.

Below: View of Pyrgos from high up.

The church of Christ in Pyrgos.

built in the 11th century a little after Episkopi Gonia. From the period 1537 - 1650, are dated the churches of Metamorphosi tou Sotira (the Transfiguration of the Saviour) or the 'Christoulaki' (Little Christ), Agios Yiannis o Theologos (the Divine), Agia Theodosia and the subterranean Agios Nikolaos tou Kissira. The church of Eisodion tou Theotokou (the Presentation of the Virgin) was built between 1650 and 1664, Agia Aikaterini in 1660, Agios Georgios in 1680, Agios Dimitrios and Taxiarchis Michael (Archangel Michael) in 1690, Agios Nikolaos in 1700... and that is far from a complete list. The number does, however, become less daunting when one thinks that the island has a total of 352 churches. In Pyrgos, the visitor will find everything he needs for his stay and the village has the further advantage of being close to Perissa and Kamari.

Profitis Ilias

From Pyrgos square we take the road which climbs, for a distance of 4.2 km, towards the Profitis Ilias monastery. Those who are fond of mountainous walks may prefer to take the old stepped path.

We are climbing up to the highest point on the island. The landscape changes continuously according to the direction of the road and the view out over the caldera becomes increasingly spectacular. The crystalline outcrops on the mountain remind us that this is not only the highest point on the island but also the oldest, one of the very few which predate the volcano (see page 18).

At the end of this route is the Profitis Ilias monastery (altitude 567 m). The monastery of Profitis Ilias tou Thesvitou was built at the beginning of the 18th century, between 1711 and 1724, and was originally smaller than it is today. The extension was made one hundred years later, in the middle of the 19th century, by order of King Othion –the first king of modern Greece– who visited the island and was enchanted by the landscape.

3

Originally, the monastery was coenobite with strict rules and until 1853 entry was strictly forbidden to women. Nowadays the number of monks has fallen to such a low level that the term 'coenobite' has very little meaning. The monastery was rich both in land and intellectual activity.

We visit the church first and then continue to the museum which consists of two parts: one **ecclesiastical** and the other **folk**. The ecclesiastical part contains all of the monastery's holy relics: Cretan icons of the 15th century, folk art from the 18th century, holy vessels, crucifixes, chalices, holy relics, vestments –amongst which is the mitre of the Patriarch, Gregorius V– manuscript codices of the 8th century, patriarchal seals and epistles as well as Turkish firmans granting privileges to the monastery. In the library, besides the more modern works, there are also 1,200 old volumes of religious content.

The folk section of the museum is made up of those parts of the monastery devoted to the domestic chores. All the fittings, with traditional furniture and tools are still there and it is easy for the visitor to imagine the daily round of toil for the islanders of the 19th century. Finally, the monastery also houses the private collection of P. Nomikos which contains woven goods, embroideries, china and paintings from old mansions of the island. And again, for those who are fond of walking, a path begins at the monastery and leads east to Mesa Vouno, from where it forks: one branch leading to Perissa and the other to Kamari. Stout footwear is necessary for one's feet sink immediately into the eroded ground and walking becomes very difficult.

1. The ornate wooden iconostasis from the katholikon. Work of Demis Langadas (1836).
2. The monastery courtyard. In the foreground is a font of whitish marble.
3. The monastery gatehouse under the belfry.
4, 5. Rooms in the folklore museum.

Route 4

Kamari - Mesa Vouno

Fira - Mesa Gonia - Kamari - Mesa Vouno
Total route: 25.2 km

The bishop's residence at Mesa Gonia.

The aims of today's route are to visit a Byzantine monument, visit ancient Thera and have a meal and a swim at Kamari beach. One should set aside one and a half hours for these visits and to allow plenty of time, one should count on leaving in the morning and returning in the afternoon. The first part of this route is the same as the start of Route 3, which we follow up to the fourth kilometre where we meet the turning for Kamari and bear right.

We pass by the turning for Vothonas on the right. In the direction of Pyrgos, we meet the side road to Mesa Gonia, which we also pass and continue up to the 6.2 km stage, at which point we encounter, on our right, the main road to Mesa Gonia which we follow for one kilometre. At the start of this road we have, directly in front of us, the village of **Mesa Gonia** or **Episkopi Gonia**. There are not many inhabitants, yet this is one of the villages in which most stock breeding on Santorini is practised. After 400 metres, we reach the entrance to the village and turn left. We go on for a further 700 metres before reaching the most important Byzantine monument on Santorini, the church of Episkopi Gonia, built in the 11th century.

Today, Episkopi Gonia is nothing but a small chapel with picturesque architecture. Once, however, it was a place of great glory and was the cause of many years of conflict between Orthodox and Catholics. The Panagia of Gonia dedicated to Kimissi tis Theotokos (the Assumption of the Virgin), appears to have been founded by the Emperor Alexius I Comnenus (1081 - 1118) and to become the seat of the bishop of Santorini. However, when the Franks arrived in 1204, the chapel was turned over to the Catholics. In 1537, when the Turks conquered the island, the Orthodox took advantage of the situation to take a part of it back; but of course only a part. The church estates were shared out

between the Orthodox and Catholics and both had the right to use the church for worship. That was when the conflicts began: who would be the first to hold their service on August 15th? (the feast day of Panagia), and who would be the first to celebrate vespers on the previous day? Disputes which sometimes involved a resort to arms. In 1768, the Patriarch and the Sultan brought an end to all the bickering by banning the Catholics from using the church. When the modern Greek state was formed, the church property was gradually appropriated and all that remains of it today is the site of the church and its surrounding courtyard. The building we see today does not have exactly the same design as the church of the 11th century as additions have been made from time to time, among which are the bell-tower and the exterior staircase.

The details of the building have also disappeared since it was unfortunately plastered and whitewashed at some point –its red roof tiles not excepted! What has remained untouched is the carved iconostasis made of light blue marble with a white grain.

Kamari

Ten kilometres southwest of Fira we reach Kamari. As we continue a little further, we come on our left to the main road that leads to the beach of Kamari.

In ancient times, Kamari was the port of Thera (which we shall soon be visiting at Mesa Vouno) and was called Oia. A number of archaeological finds have been discovered here. One of the most noteworthy sites of Kamari is the church of 'Myrtidiotissa'.

Today, Kamari is one of the coastal settlements of Santorini which has grown from nothing and has developed at an amazing rate. Before the earthquake, this area was empty; there was no settlement, no houses; nothing. Today it is a large village which grows larger and more developed every year.

Kamari owes this rapid development to the sea and its beach. It is an endless east-facing beach with coarse black sand and crystal clear water, which is protected to the south by the vertical mass of Mesa Vouno. The only thing to be aware of is that the sea rapidly becomes very deep, quicker than one might expect on a sandy beach and there are strong cross currents which form dangerous whirlpools.

One more of the advantages of Kamari, and one which makes it almost unique on Santorini, besides its wonderful beaches, is that there are underground sources of water. The visitor can also find everything he needs for his stay here: from large hotels with swimming pools to rooms for rent, restaurants, fish tavernas, cinemas, discos and a camping ground.

Mesa Vouno

We return to the point at which we left the main road (7.9 km) and continue towards Mesa Vouno. The road winds up the rocky mass with narrow hairpin bends but is quite passable.

The climb is three kilometres long and is so steep that Kamari begins to appear below us as if we were seeing it from an aeroplane. On the side of the hill to the right of our road, we can also see the old road which climbed the hill with the steps.

At 10.9 km, we reach a piece of flat ground 264 metres above sea level, this being the 'neck' between the main mountainous mass, with its peak at the Profitis Ilias monastery and a second, lower mountainous mass to the east. This 'neck' is lower and is called Mesa Vouno.

Ancient Thera is on the western side of Mesa Vouno –right in front of us that is– and the 'neck' on which we stand is called Sellada. Looking towards the entrance to the archaeological site, we have on our right the start of the path to Perissa, which we can see from above. On our left is Kamari and the road by which we came. Behind us begins a path leading up to Profitis Ilias (see route 3, page 97).

Perissa: with the protection that the huge rock of Mesa Vouno gives, you will have one of the most wonderful swims of your holiday.

Route 5

Fira - Perissa

**Main route: Fira - Messaria - Vothonas
Megalochori - Emboreio - Perissa**

Secondary routes: **a) Karterados
Exo Gialos Karteradou b) Athinios**

All the routes we suggest here end at one
beach or another and so this is a day's outing to
be combined with a swim. The main route leads
to the southern beaches. The first secondary
route leads to the east coast and the second to
the west. Thus the beach from which one is going to swim can be chosen on the basis of the direction of the wind.

*The villages of Vothonas and Messaria as they
can be seen from the road.*

Main Route

From Fira we take the road with the
Eucalyptus trees. This is the southern part of
Santorini's main road axis, which ends at
Perissa after passing –directly or indirectly–
through most of the villages on the island.
After about four kilometres, we reach **Messaria**,
an inland village which stands at the
crossroads of the island's main roads and this,
despite its distance from the coast, is enough
to explain the large number of small hotels,
bars etc. which are to be seen as one enters
the village. Messaria is agricultural, its
Co-operative was one of the island's most
active and even today the village produces a
major proportion of Santorinian wine which can
still be sampled in the two small wineries.
What really demonstrates, quite sensationally,
the vigour of the villagers of Messaria is their
eye clinic, founded in 1929.

At the beginning of the 20th century, some 80% of the island's inhabitants suffered from trachoma, an illness which leads to blindness. The initiative was taken by individuals to fight this and the 'Agia Varvara Eye Clinic' was founded. By 1948 the number of people suffering from trachoma had fallen to 19%. In 1954, however, the clinic was closed because it was under private law.

We continue along our road which now begins to rise towards Pyrgos with many bends.

Immediately after the intersection lies the village of **Vothonas**. With a population of 436, it looks like a continuation of Messaria on the other side of the road. Interesting are the skafta houses and also the churches of Agia Triada, Agia Anna and of Panagia.

1. The village of Vothonas.

2. The vines are protected by the people of Santorini in a very clever way from the winds. They are coiled in a unique way and look like baskets.

3. Goulas in Emboreio, one of the surviving Medieval strongholds of the island.

4. View of Emboreio.

If the time of year is one at which the vines happen to be in leaf, it is worth stopping for a moment on our way up the hill in order to see the clever way the islanders have found to protect their crop from the wind.

Each vine plant is pruned in such a way as to form one huge stem, which is then trained to grow in coils round and round its root, just as one might coil a hose. When the vine is in leaf, the new twigs emerge from the coil and bear their fruit, but only a relatively small area of the surface of the vine is exposed to the wind. In the winter, it looks, from a distance, as if the whole plain is scattered with woven baskets (see page 38).

At the 6.8 km stage is a crossroads leading to the top of the hill. To the right is the chapel of Agios Andreas, whilst the road to Pyrgos is on the left. At 7.7 kilometres, to our right is a road leading to Athinios (see below, Secondary Route b). From here on, the road begins to run gently down to the southern plain of the island. At 8.5 kilometres, on our left we meet the turning to **Megalochori**. It is a traditional settlement with two large hotel complexes and only 335 inhabitants as well as the well known winery of Boutaris. Ten kilometres along, on our right is the turning to Akrotiri and the archaeological site (see pages 68 - 78).

Twelve kilometres from Fira, we pass through the village of **Emboreio** or Nimborio. This is the largest village in the south of the island, built in the midst of the plain of the same name, and is picturesque with narrow alleyways and neighbourhoods. The name of the village and the ruined windmills which can be seen on the hill opposite, bear witness to its former activities. Today, of course, the people of Emboreio are also involved in fishing. The 'harbour' of the village is at Perissa where the residents have their fishing boats moored.

During the period of Venetian Occupation, Emboreio had one of the island's five large strongholds as well as a goulas (fortified mansion), but of these, only ruins survive today.

Perissa

At the fifteenth kilometre of the main route we find Perissa and reach the end of our route. There are three elements in the view which spreads out before us: the fine black sand of the beach, the rocky mass of Mesa Vouno and the church of Perissa, the Timios Stavros (Holy Cross). Mesa Vouno, which rises almost vertically at the eastern end of the beach, has nothing in common with the type of rock to which Santorini has so far accustomed us. It is one of the peaks of ancient Aegeis which remained above the surface of the sea when the Aegean was formed and consequently was there before the volcano erupted and before Santorini came into being.

The Timios Stavros church, the largest on Santorini and a place of pilgrimage for the islanders, comes as something of a surprise, seemingly rising out
of the sand at a spot where one would expect at most a little chapel.

-There is of course also a small chapel at Perissa, that of Agia Irini, built at the end of the 16th or beginning of the 17th century and which many claim is the origin of the name of the island. This honour, however, is disputed –perhaps with some justice– by the Agia Irini on Thirassia.

The beach of Perissa, one of the most frequented on the island, has all the necessary facilities: restaurants, refreshment bars, etc.

The south coast of the island, beginning to the east at Mesa Vouno, runs west almost as far as Akrotiri, frequently changing names. As a continuation of the beach at Perissa we find **Perivolos** which, together with Agios Georgios, forms a beach four kilometres long which stretches around to Vlychada. The thin sand and the clean sea give the visitor the opportunity to enjoy water sports and good food in the fish tavernas along the beach. The beaches of **Agios Giorgis tou Thalassinou** (of Sailors), or 'Thalassitis' and **Vlychada** follow, where the geological upheavals from the eruption of the volcano gave this area a lunar apperance.

Finally, there follows the beach of **Exomytis** where, after the completion of the marina, a large development of the area is expected because it will house many tourist vessels. The other beaches, lying still further west, are reached from other roads and are not covered by this route, they are all fine beaches and much less crowded. They are not reached directly from Perissa, though access is via the side roads we encountered on our way from Emboreio. Therefore, we must turn back.

Above: Panoramic view of Perissa.
Right: View of Karterados.

Secondary Routes

Fira - Karterados - Exo Gialos Karteradou

From Fira we follow the main route until the 1.3 km stage where we find the second side road to Karterados and turn left. The road leads to the southern part of the village, crossing it at one point.

Karterados is most striking for its position. Once one has gotten used to the landscape of Santorini, with its villages usually built at commanding points or on plains, Karterados comes as a surprise, hidden in a gully with the roofs of the houses at the same level as the road. Of course its position protects it from the north winds which pass literally over the top of it given that the gully runs east-west. Another possible reason for the selection of its position, may be that the gully provides two almost vertical banks which are ideal for the construction of skafta houses.

After the square, it is worth stopping to observe the three churches on the left. In the middle, the main church of the village, the Analypsi (Ascension), is an example of the western style imported from Italy as it was adapted in the Cyclades. There is a dome on top and there are also two square tower-like belfries on the façade, left and right of the main entrance.

Another indicative element of the foreign provenance, is the colour: the main exterior surfaces are ochre, combined with a little white on the mouldings, the window sills and the door and window frames. The dome is neither the pure light blue which is the custom on the island, nor white. It is the light turquoise of tarnished copper and, together with the ochre and white makes a fine composition in pastel shades. The Analypsi of Karterados is reminiscent of the cathedral of Fira, the old Panagia of Belonia, as it was before the earthquakes.

Right and left of the Analypsi, as we see them from the road, are the churches of Eisodion tis Theotokos (Presentation of the Virgin) and

Agios Nikolaos, built in the Santorinian style and creating a sharp contrast.

They are rectangular basilicas with semicircular vaulted roofs and front walls extending upwards as a pediment, above the level of the vault, to form a flat triangular 'belfry'. There are three openings, rising to semicircular arches, in the base of the triangle, and a fourth at the point of the triangle. In each opening there is a bell. Naturally, these churches are painted white.

Leaving the village, on the left there is a tennis court. The sight of the tennis court, so suddenly, with the absolute clarity of its lines and colours in the sandy, almost lunar, landscape, sets one thinking, involuntarily, of Dali. One could quite easily make the scene the subject of a painting entitled 'The Oasis'.

After continuing east for about one kilometre from the end of Karterados, we come to **Exo Gialos tou Karteradou**. The beach is beautiful with black sand and large pebbles and some tamarisks for shade. When there is not a north wind, this area is ideal for swimming as it is the nearest beach to Fira.

Fira - Athinios

From Fira, we follow the main route until the 7.7 km stage at which point we encounter a road to the right in the direction of the caldera which takes us to Athinios, the port of Santorini.
The road winds steeply down for three kilometres and there are many bends.

This road is the only one on the island which leads to a point at which ships can anchor.
Its construction, therefore, was decisive in the modernization of the island. The cliff we arc descending is, like Mesa Vouno at Perissa, a remnant of Aegeis, with a light-coloured crystalline rock formation different from the familiar volcanic landscape of the island. When we reach the bottom, at the bay of Athinios, we will find a few small houses, restaurants, bars –and the jetty; perhaps the most precious thing on the island –its lifeline to the outside world. To the right of the jetty is an attractive little beach with pebbles.

One last swim is always the best thing to do while waiting for the ship to appear.

The port of Fira, Athinios, from high up.

Route 6
Fira - Akrotiri

Our aim on this route is to come to grips with the ancient civilization of Santorini as it was before the eruption of 1450 BC and the sinking of half the island.

For the first ten kilometres of this route, we shall follow the Perissa road, in other words, we go past the turning for Pyrgos and that for Athinios and continue for a further two and a half kilometres.

At the tenth kilometre there is a turning on our right which leads to Akrotiri and following this, we meet a chapel, further along on our left.

Across from the chapel, a road begins which leads down into the caldera and after about one hundred metres encounters the sea.

At the thirteenth kilometre, after bypassing the side road to our right which leads to the village of Akrotiri, we follow the road which ends up at the furthest point of the cape where the lighthouse stands. Two hundred metres further on, we see Akrotiri which was one of the island's five strongholds during the Frankish Occupation. The village would be an isolated spot lying off the main road axis of the island, if the neighbouring archaeological site did not attract people and trade continuously.

After a hundred metres, we turn left and head in the direction of the southern beach.

At the fourteenth kilometre, our route has almost reached the beach. The entrance to the archaeological site is on our left (see Archaeological Sites, page 68).

If you really want to enjoy your swim, continue just a little further. Directly opposite the entrance to the archaeological site, a track begins which heads west following the line of the coast.

At fifteen kilometres from Fira, we reach the very picturesque spot known as **Mavro Rachidi**. We can distinguish it by the black and reddish rocks which run down to the sea and by the chapel of Agios Nikolas which strikes a contrast with its dazzling white against the dark background of the rocks. After crossing the courtyard of the chapel, we take the path which brings us to a marvellous sandy beach –the red beach– where we will have our swim. This beach can also be reached by boat from the beach directly after the archaeological site. We return to the point at which we left the asphalt road (the 13 km stage of our route).

One kilometre further along, at the fourteenth kilometre, there is a turning to the left. The track leads to the western entrance of Akrotiri. Further on, on our left, exactly on the bend, is the chapel of Agios Yiannis. At fifteen kilometres, to the left is a turning which leads to the church of Panagia. From here there is a minor road which also leads to the Agios Yiannis chapel. At the next junction, the track leads south and itself has a road left after a further one hundred metres. If we go straight on, we will come, after about one kilometre, to the underground church of the Taxiarchi (the Archangel). If we take the side road, we shall come out either at the church of Panagia (in front and to the left of us), or at that of Christos (Christ) (to our right after about 1 km).

Sixteen kilometres along, to the left is a track for Mesa Pigadi, which takes us to the southern **beach of the cape** (about 1 km). Further on, we see another track which ends at the caldera after about one kilometre.

Finally, at eighteen kilometres we come to the end of the road and find the lighthouse, which is, generally speaking, not open to visitors.

1. The chapel of Agios Nikolaos
dazzlingly white against the dark rocks.

2. The beach of the cape.

3. The black and red pebbles look like pearls on the beaches of Santorini.

4. The lighthouse stands out at the island's furthest extremity.

5. The red beach that looks like an unrealistic landscape with the surronding imposing rocks.

Route 7
A Tour of the Caldera

Part of today's route will involve the use of the **boats** which make the trip around the caldera. Before starting, find out the times of the trips and, if you wish, pre-purchase tickets from one of the agencies in Fira.

There are normally two trips a day, one in the morning and one in the afternoon, the morning run lasting longer. Stout walking shoes and socks are essential to permit comfortable walking on the volcano.

It is also a good idea to have a snack and a bottle of water with one, especially if taking the morning trip.

One should not miss the visit to the islands of Nea Kameni and Palaia Kameni to see the volcano. You can, if you wish, disembark on Nea Kameni and walk to the crater. It will take about thirty minutes but you should have suitable shoes because the ground is warm. This excursion will be by boat from the bay of Fira and takes only ten minutes. You can also choose the longer excursion which goes, not only to the volcano, but also to the little island of Aspronisi, the picturesque little island of Thirassia (both are remnants from the old Santorini that drowned) and to beautiful Oia.

Donkey rides, or "Gaïdourokavalaria" as the locals call them, on the 'dromos tou Gialou'.

Fira - Mesa Gialos

We start an hour before the time the boat leaves, from the crossroads of Mich. Danezi and Ypapantis streets and take Sp. Marinatou street, directly in front of us. The first part of the route is the descent of the cliff down to sea level on foot. The road spirals down, consisting of 587 broad steps. Each straight section between two bends is known as a vena and some of them have names: Alonakia (the little threshing floors), Gria Spilia (the old caves), etc. At one time this road-way was the only access which connected the island with the ships, and mules were the only means of transport for people and goods. To-day, with the road to Athinios, this road, the 'dro-mos tou Gialou' (Gialos road), has remained one of the most picturesque elements of the island because of its setting and because the road ends in a very beautiful bay. Cruise ships continue to land their passengers at Mesa Gia-los and the cable-car also leads there.

At the start of our route, we walk among the houses most of which are in the lower part of Fira, and have been converted into souvenir shops, coffee shops and restaurants.

As these houses thin out, we gradually realise that the walls of the crater are all around us.

Now we are seeing the crater not from above but from inside and we can stop to observe the various geological strata of which it consists: brown, reddish and grey/black, and as we descend the volcano becomes larger and larger until it completely fills the horizon.

In about twenty minutes we reach the bottom. Mesa Gialos is a picturesque little port with its small houses, coffee shops and jetty. It would be just like every other little port in the Cyclades if it were not for the fearsome cliff which surrounds it and if that cliff did not continue into the sea.

119

On the northern side of the bay, the
yellowish cliff plunging down from above has
been eroded at its base by the sea which has
thus formed a number of caves. They look
rather like broken-down skafta houses which
have sunk into the water and they have given
this corner of the bay its name – **Trypes**,
meaning holes. The starting point for the
cable-car is near here.

We have a little time to walk around the
south side of the bay. The first place we come
to is Limanaki, formed by a small jetty running
parallel to the shore behind which are moored
the boats which once brought passengers
ashore from the ferries and now, motorized, do
the same job for the cruise liners.

Still further back is the picturesque chapel of
Agios Nikolas. Continuing, we come to a path
which leads to a small jetty at the southernmost
end of the bay. The area around this jetty is
known as **Lazareta**.

Swimming is possible here, the water being
relatively safe for some way out. Care should be
taken though not to get too far from the shore
and not to swim when there is a strong wind.
We return to the main jetty of Gialos and board
the boat.

Our boat starts off in a westerly direction
and heads for the northern harbour of the
volcano. Looking back, we get a general idea of
the walls of the caldera with the brilliant white
fringe of Fira on top. To the right of this appears
Balades, the place where pumice is mined, and
its installations for loading the ships.

Five or six minutes after the boat has left,
the depth of the sea beneath us is the same as
the height of Fira above Gialos: 300 metres,
give or take. After this, the water becomes
much shallower, especially to the left of the
boat as we go forwards. At this point there is an
outcrop of the seabed which permits the larger
ships to fall back upon it and this is where the
cruise ships stop. The spot is known as
'Bagoss'.

1

2

Volcano - Nea Kameni

Now we are close to the volcano and the first mass of black lava can be seen on the right. It can easily be seen from the appearance of the lava that the black material issued forth from the ground in viscous form, cooling suddenly and retaining the form it had when it reached the surface. It gives one a fair idea of what Hell must be like...

This lava is relatively recent and dates only from the 1925 - 26 eruption. As we enter the little harbour in which we shall disembark, the water begins to take on a green opaque look produced by the sulphur. Later, we shall have the opportunity to swim around our moored boat and will be able to confirm for ourselves that the water is lukewarm.

For the moment we leave the boat and take the uphill path which leads to the crater. The whole trip, there and back, takes about an hour. There is nothing but lava.

The crater is perhaps the least awe-inspiring feature of the volcano. It resembles a gigantic basin of pumice on whose rim we stand. Not, of course, that the crater does not provoke a certain measure of awe, the proof of which can be felt in the silence which is suddenly apparent and the fact that no one dares to go down to the bottom. Around us, sulphurous gases are emitted at a number of points. At other points, the ground and stones are hot. Lifting up some of the stones, you will see, on the lower surface, the bright yellow crystals of sulphur which cover it.

We return to the shore and stay a short while for a swim; a blessing after the dust, earth and heat of the volcano.

1, 2. The picturesque bay of Mesa Gialos which is special because of the cliff that surrounds it.
3. In the bay of the volcano you will have the finest swim in the lukewarm, green, opaque waters.

3   *Leaving the volcano behind, our boat now heads for **Thirassia**, the independent part of the caldera which forms its northwestern wall. During the voyage we shall be able to observe the two separate islands which make up the volcano: **Nea Kameni** which we have just been visiting, and behind it long and narrow, **Palaia Kameni**, which was already fully formed by 1508 (see table of eruptions, page 19).*

Continuing our route, our boat will cross the strait which separates Thirassia from Apano Meria (just over a mile) and will stop at one of the two bays, Ammoudi or Armeni. Apano Meria, however, is one of the most interesting points of Santorini and we can get a general view of its landscape from the sea.

After Apano Meria, our return journey begins. Our boat crosses the caldera from north to south and we have the chance to see all the wild beauty of the strata of which Santorini is made up with the central point the rock of Skaros rising up like an enormous stone castle in the middle of the sea. The little white dot to

4   *be discerned high up on Skaros 'is the Theoskepasti chapel.*

Upon arriving back in Mesa Gialos, we have two possibilities for climbing back up to Fira: the donkeys or the cable-car. Perhaps we may choose the donkeys this time as being more colourful and choose the cable-cars on another occasion for a second –and impressive– trip to Mesa Gialos and a quick swim at Lazareta.

1, 2, 3. The walk on the volcano creates fear and fright, seeing on one side the black stones of lava and on the other side the sulphur coming from the crater which is still steaming.

4. The tour of the caldera gives one the opportunity to see a wonderful view.

Thirassia

1

Thirassia is the second largest island of the complex which forms the caldera (5.7 km long and 2.7 km wide at its widest point). There are, however, only 245 inhabitants. Isolated from the main mass of Santorini, Thirassia has not followed the rapid course of its development and organized visits to the island are short. The island hides many pleasant surprises for the visitor who wants to get to know it better.
The population of Thirassia consists mainly of seamen and farmers who till the fertile western plain of the island and produce grapes, tomatoes, favas and barley. The main settlement is built on top of the cliff which is not so high at this point: 145 steps are sufficient to bring one to the top. The settlement itself reminds one of other villages of Santorini: the same cobbled streets, the same architecture, the same view.
If you like bread go to the traditional bakery, or visit the picturesque tavernas if there is eating time. The descent of the road leads to Potamos (93 inhabitants) rooted in a ravine with colourful houses and many skafta, the churches of Agios Dimitris and Panagia Giatrissa which are honoured with special devotion by all people of Thirassia.

In the northern part of the island is Riva, an excellent sandy beach with traditional tavernas almost in the sea and the picturesque chapel of Agia Irini. As many say, this little chapel of Agia Irini gave Santorini its name, contesting for the honour with the Agia Irini at Perissa (see route 5, page 107).

Continuing along the coastal asphalt road, we come to Agrilia, holding in her embrace an invaluable treasure, Panagia tou Lagadi (of the Gorge) or Panagia Eisodion (of the Presentation), with rare architecture and sculpted decorations showing double-headed eagles, angels and other representations.

1. The bay of Korfos.
2. The village of Manolas.
3. A view of Thirassia.

2

3

If we continue south and before reaching the edge of the island, we can stop at Keras, located at the foot of Profitis Ilias, and look at the stacked skafta houses that take us centuries back to when the people were taking their animals for protection from invasions whilst, in their front part, the beds for the people were dug out to the right and left. On the right part of the island there are long narrow parallel masses of white lava with striking ravines formed among them. All these shapes are a result of the repeated eruptions of the volcano which threw lava to the long and narrow backside of Thirassia. The winds, however, at the first opportunity, pushed the lava to the right of the island and so the above mentioned masses were formed in the valley down to sea level. The villages of Agrilia and Potamos were later built in these ravines.

Continuing further on we will reach the monastery of Kimisseos (the Assumption), nestling with traditional craftsmanship at the southernmost end of the island, sheltered from the winds. Before entering the monastery, marvel at the view that stretches out before you and you will see why the island was named Strongyle. A complete circle from Oia to Akrotiri appears with the inside full of water. In the centre the volcano, and on the edge Aspronisi, looking like a huge passenger ship entering the port. With this picture in our minds, we reach the courtyard of the monastery which has eighteen cells, and was built with remarkable skill, according to the island traditions, by 1851. It is a compact circular structure with the church of Megalochori in the centre. Opposite us is a marble sarcophagus and the Russian iconostasis is decorated in gold with the Evangelists and the Apostles Peter and Paul, a fine Russian hagiograph which shows the marks of the holiness of these persons. On the right is the icon of Christ and on the left that of Panagia. Admiring this iconostasis one realizes why a hiero-monk sold all of his possessions and went to Russia to bring it to the monastery himself.

Coming out of the sacred place, the cape of Kimino is distinguishable opposite. Slowly, we take the way back and after a few minutes the

A very beautiful little chapel on Thirassia.

central village of the island, Manolas appears, as if riding on the back of Thirassia. It is an impressive village with its white and blue colours, and the harmony of its houses which all bind together and resist the vehemence of the winds. In the centre, the magnificent church of Agios Konstantinos (guardian angel of the island), overlooks the village. Down at the bottom, on the left, is the port of Korfos which served all the sailors of Thirassia who returned home with their merchandise. At sea level on the tip of Korfos, one can see the cape of Simantiri, whose vertical mass, up to the white lava, has exactly the same composition as the opposite one of Oia. Major proof for the separation of Thirassia from Santorini after the eruption. Here ends our tour on the forgotten island of Thirassia, which lives in the shadows because the light is on Santorini. Visit it and you are certain to be charmed by its special churches and its masses of white lava. The boat trip does not usually include time for a walk up to Thirassia and a visit to the whole island. What is most usual is for there to be a stop at the bay for a swim and a snack on the beach near the white chapel of Zoodochos Pigi.

The bay of Korfos.

Texts: I. ALEXAKIS
Artistic Editor: EVI DAMIRI
Translation: IDA ORNSTEIN, PHILIP RAMP

Colour Separation - Printing: M. Toubis S.A.